HENRY IRVING AND *THE BELLS*

Sir Henry Irving as Mathias in The Bell

HENRY IRVING
AND
THE BELLS

Irving's personal script
of the play by LEOPOLD LEWIS

edited and introduced by DAVID MAYER

with a memoir by ERIC JONES-EVANS

Etienne Singla's original musical score
arranged by NIGEL GARDNER

and a Foreword by MARIUS GORING

MANCHESTER UNIVERSITY PRESS

First published 1980 by MANCHESTER UNIVERSITY PRESS
Oxford Road, Manchester M13 9PL

British Library Cataloguing in Publication Data

Henry Irving and 'The bells'.
  1. Lewis, Leopold. Bells
  I. Mayer, David   II. Jones-Evans, Eric
  III. Lewis, Leopold. Bells
  822'.8   PR4886.L8B42

ISBN 0-7190-0798-4

Printed in Great Britain by
Butler & Tanner Ltd,
Frome and London

CONTENTS

ILLUSTRATIONS

vii

The frontispiece portrait, the Costume studies and the Testimonial were lent to the Russell-Cotes Art Gallery and Museum by Eric Jones-Evans, and the Statuette by Laurence Irving.

ACKNOWLEDGEMENTS

One of the final pleasures of editorship is thanking those persons whose generous assistance materially aided the shape and content of a published work. *Henry Irving and 'The Bells'* would have fared less well without such sure help, and I am proud to acknowledge my gratitude and indebtedness to the following institutions, associates, and loved ones. From both the University of Manchester and the British Academy I received funds to cover some travel and research costs. To Marius Goring I am twice grateful: first, for allowing me to reproduce Henry Irving's typescript of *The Bells*, the centre of this volume, and, second, for his continuing interest and moral support for this project. The staff of Samuel French Ltd., George Rowell, Dr Louis James, and Professor Michael Booth helped to answer queries about the nature of the text of *The Bells* first published by French's. Dr Ward Gardner and the Solent Sinfonia, in recording the full score to *The Bells* turned speculation about Etienne Singla's score into audible actuality. To Sarah Woodcock of the Theatre Museum, Michael Hall of the Audio-Visual Unit in Bristol University's Department of Drama, and Graham Teasdill of the Russell-Cotes Art Gallery and Museum, Bournemouth, I am indebted for assistance in locating, identifying, and obtaining many of the illustrations found on the pages to follow. John Parkinson, an accomplished stage designer in his own right, aided in translating Irving's notes and Dr Jones-Evans's recollections into reliable floorplans of the settings. Helen Day, George Taylor, and Helen Shaw gave invaluable help in collating, assessing, and transcribing text. I have benefited from the advice and guidance of John Banks of Manchester University Press and from help given by Richard Bebb and Stanley MacKenzie. Finally, I am deeply and forever grateful to my daughters Cassandra, Lise, and Catherine. Their enthusiasm, warmth, love and constancy, as much as their practical assistance and sustained interest, are part and parcel of this book. I hope they and the others mentioned above recognise the degree of their wholehearted contributions and my unstinting gratitude.

D.M.

FOREWORD

'There is no such thing', said Benjamin Britten, irately, when told, after recording one of his works for posterity, that it was the 'definitive performance'. The scholarly investigation in this book demonstrates the truth of his statement, for as each musical performance varies according to the idiosyncrasy of the performers, mood of the listeners, acoustic and temperature of the concert hall, so is a play, in theatres of widely differing size and atmosphere, performed by varying actors, in words requiring personal interpretation, even more subject to change. If Beethoven did not set down a note of the Kreutzer Sonata's second movement before the two giants had performed it together, small wonder that Leopold Lewis's *Bells* did not exist before Irving played it.

Written descriptions of acting performances seldom succeed in arousing the reader; when their moment has gone, they fade into the mist of old, jumbled letters and photographs; faces look beyond us from a past as distant as tomorrow. But we are fortunate as regards Irving: we already have the most evocative description ever written of an actor by his pupil, Gordon Craig, and one of the finest and most knowledgeable biographies by his grandson, Laurence Irving. Craig ends his description in these words: 'I can write no more; you may perhaps have felt something. I don't know—but, if you did, I know it was one thousandth part of what we felt. As we watched this figure we felt as silent and as still as when we hear of things too sad to realise; and when it was over and we might move, we knew that this was the finest point that the craft of acting could reach.'[1]

If only we knew more! Peering through a glass darkly, might we not catch a reflection of lightning flashes like those that Hazlitt saw? Now we have this book in which Eric Jones-Evans gives a detailed commentary on an authenticated text of the play about what happened, what Irving did—during the one performance he witnessed—he wastes no words in trying to say how Irving did it. Nigel Gardner describes the music of the melodrama, and David Mayer annotates the various extant texts in terms of these comments.

Setting aside false hopes of finding a 'definitive edition' of *The Bells*, upon which of the thousand or more performances referred to in this book should one focus the imagination? On the one of 25 November 1871, when a revolution in the English Theatre took place and an audience, already weary of stereotyped melodrama in Red Barns and Barber Shops, first peered into the labyrinths of Dostoyevsky and Freud? Historical details are plentiful. At 10.30 a.m., Irving was at Drury Lane to perform his Jingle, with Samuel Phelps as Sir Pertinax Mac-sycophant, and many others in a multi-coloured Farewell Benefit of Mr H. Boleno, a much loved, retiring Clown.[2] Unfortunately, after some hours had passed, three items (including Pickwick) remained unperformed: 'Time, the in-exorable, cried "No More", and the National Anthem was played among some marks of disapprobation....'[3] By 4.00 p.m. Irving was back at the Lyceum experimenting with sleigh-bells. In the evening, after his first performance of Mathias, he played the same Jingle he had missed in the morning. The pro-prietor of the *Daily Telegraph* said to his critic, Clement Scott: 'Tonight I have seen a great actor at the Lyceum—a great actor. There was a poor house. Write about him so that everyone shall know he is great.' The success was unforeseen by the management and, late that night, somebody was sent to buy champagne. His wife was anxious that he 'might be boring the company ... In the brougham as they drove towards Fulham, he was in the best of spirits ... "Are you going on making a fool of yourself like this all your life?" she asked. They were crossing Hyde Park Corner. Irving told the driver of the brougham to stop. Without a word he got out and left his wife to continue the journey alone. He never returned to his home and he never spoke to her again.'[4]

Hawes Craven had conjured up the stage sets from old pieces of scenery of other plays (including a beautiful but inappropriate back-cloth) and they remained basically the same until Irving died. Probably all the music composed by M. Singla for the previous Paris production was played. The text was close to that of the manuscript passed by the Lord Chamberlain; the 'Vision' at the end of Act I replaced the entry of the Polish Jew in the French version. Irving must have fought hard enough to achieve that without attempting further changes. The critics (needless to say) attacked Lewis for this abuse of the original, French play (poor fellow! He would never have had the theatrical wit to think up Irving's amendment for himself) and made objections to certain points in Irving's per-formance, complaining, in particular, about 'longueur' in the Dream sequence. Was the performance only one of young promise, or did it achieve mature greatness as the proprietor of the *Telegraph* suggested? Was his first entrance applauded? Certainly the Garrick Club did not think so. He was blackballed and had to wait two years before becoming worthy of membership.

Or does one fix on the performance of 1892, when the Lyceum company pre-sented Irving with an illuminated address of congratulation on his theatrical revolution twenty-one years before? None of the original company was still with him and some of the signatories, including Gordon Craig, were not even born in '71.

The famous Hawes Craven backdrop was still extant—and the problem it represented. In the Polish Jew's winter, the half-starved Mathias, wife and child barely eked out their existence in the ramshackle village inn, and, when the play's action commences, they still use it, well refurbished for old time's sake and have built (presumably) a fine Mayor's Parlour overhead suited to the Landlord's new status, for is he not Burgomaster of the—village? Surely a Burgomaster holds municipal office? In 1871, the Manager, Bateman, was almost as impecunious as the young Mathias; would he not have baulked at paying for a new backdrop portraying—nobody was sure what? He would have been as vehement as Lilian Baylis, years later at the Old Vic, who, when asked to provide missing scenery for *Hamlet*, declared: 'We've a couple of old flats from *Tosca* that will do nicely!' Hawes Craven had a beauty which certainly suggested the more likely neighbourhood of a Burgomaster but hardly the lonely inn visited by the Polish Jew. The fire of '98 destroyed it but not the problem.

Long before 1892, with M. Singla back in Paris, Irving would have cut the unnecessary 'incidental' music, remoulding its basic themes into the sound effects of wind and sleigh, tocsin and marriage-bells as an organic part of the play. There is much talk of 'audience participation' today as though, like sex, it had just been invented, but it was an integral part of Irving's theatre: when the sleigh-bells are first mentioned by Mathias they are audible to him only, the audience shares his friends' puzzlement; as the sound is picked up from the far distance, they catch his anxiety of approaching danger, and horror in the sudden realisation that only they and Mathias are aware of it, while the others remain unmoved: suspension of disbelief is complete. Technically, this is not easy to achieve: in Birmingham, say, the balance of sound is right; while in Leeds Bram Stoker might protest, 'Too loud!' 'Nonsense,' Irving would reply, 'the bells are hardly audible from the gallery.' 'From the stalls it's like a post-horn announcing the Jew's arrival!'

All the official changes to Lewis's text would have been made—it is not surprising that Lewis ignored them when giving the play to French's for publication; he is not the only author to insist on original words being preserved for posterity, no matter how inadequate performance has shown them to be. The company would be practised to the degree where every point is clear and lucid, and words fall in rhythm to the death-bell of the Dream scene and counter-rhythm to the wind at the opening of the play. That short scene without Irving was a masterpiece. Gordon Craig tells how, when he looked in at the Lyceum to snatch another glimpse of him as Mathias, he always came at the beginning to rejoice in the Company 'at its best' and the stage-hands moving silently and swiftly in soft shoes, unleashing the wind and snow as the 'hurry music' played, ready for the adroit uncleating of the horizontally divided back wall that would open its jaws and reveal the 'Vision' or release the front roller curtain, striking the boards with a thud to punctuate the ending of the act.[5] The acting, after a gentle, leisurely start, imperceptibly gained in tempo and intensity as the wind, or a sound of breaking glass added tension to the measured tale of the Polish Jew, and the play moved forward on an ever-increasing swell to the flinging open of the central door, the swirling snow outside, through which a gaunt spectre seemed to enter, so that the women half-stepped back in fear, until that voice reassured them in tones of 'Do not be afraid, it is only I!' Of course! It is Mathias, husband, father, Burgomaster, loved and revered by us all, without whom Christmas would be unthinkable! And the Symphony descends to the warm tones of its opening in preparation for the themes of mystery and terror which bring the first movement to its close.

To win suspension of disbelief, everyone must do what he has to do, everything must work as in a battle. Almost a hundred years after its first performance at the Lyceum, *The Bells* was performed at the Little Derby Playhouse; everything was on a smaller scale, but everything worked and was faithful—in its fashion; and at the end of the first act there was a silence, as there had been long ago at the Lyceum, before the applause began. A year later, when virtually the same production opened in London, Mathias stood in the wings watching the first scene. Snow was falling, not outside the windows, but through the ceiling of the Inn, and he knew, before making his first entrance, that the battle was lost. Irving Wardle wrote: what 'emerges very clearly from the Derby Playhouse revival is that it is a stunning piece of theatre'; and Eric Shorter: 'The wind machine is noisy. The walls are apt to wobble ... at Derby last year [it] seemed eminently worth while ... at a West-End theatre the effect is different.'[6]

A third performance to consider would be one towards the end of the next thirteen years and the night before his death in October 1905 when Irving played Mathias for the last time. Eric Jones-Evans saw him play in February of that year and the third act of the script published in this book was typed in that same month (the first two acts were typed previously) which gives added validity to his comments; this was the 'official' version played then—'official' because Irving had aged before his time. Beatrice Forbes-Robertson, niece of Sir Johnston and the critics' doyen, J. Knight, in her entrancing memoirs describes her first professional engagement—walking on in *The Bells* during the autumn tour of 1900: 'Irving's memory was a little uncertain ... and Ellen's [Terry]—though she was ten years his junior—extremely so. Both suffered most in the parts they had played longest ... for the constant repetition of a part involves some lack of concentration. In the midst of a too well-known line you may think—"Did I remember to turn off the gas?"—and all is lost; whereas with a new part you are every instant concentrated on your lines. So, the two great stars did not hesitate in "Robespierre", but both dried up or fluffed in "The Merchant", "The Bells" and "The Vicar" ... I have seen Ellen wander quite frankly down to the prompt-box [sic] for her line, and Irving circulate the stage like a dog on the scent of his.'[7]

This may well have been the reason for the prompt script being copied around 1904–5—or dictated to the typist by the Prompter who must have known it by heart; the original, if extant, was probably undecipherable. While preparing to perform *The Bells* at Derby in 1967, it became clear to me as Mathias that the Samuel French edition was unplayable and would have to be rewritten, and I asked Laurence Irving for help. 'There is no problem,' he said; 'I have my grandfather's version; I think it must have been made for my father [H.B.] who played it when Henry died.' Once glance was enough to convince Peter Jackson, who directed the play at Derby, that this was all that was needed; he carried it off, photographed it and distributed copies to the cast and stage management as the text to be performed. Alterations were few; the main one concerned the music Laurence had also possessed, but all trace of it was lost in the Royal Academy of Music at Marylebone, whither he thought it had gone—alas, no one knew that Eric Jones-Evans was owner of a copy in Fawley. So Mr Nicholas Smith was engaged to play Dr Zimmer, adding to his saw-bones gifts those of an amateur musician, leading the villagers in his own compositions of wedding and drinking songs and strumming on his guitar accompaniments to the wind outside and the main 'Annette' theme. How did that run? One likes to think that the Governor's kindly spirit whispered a hint in the watches of the night, for M. Singla's music was a variation of the new interpolated theme: an old German carol, *Winterrose*—

There is a rose that sprang
Out of the gentle earth,
For as our Fathers sang
A rose was our Lord's birth;
A little, tender flower
All in the snow of winter
Born at the midnight hour.

Why were so many stage directions added in Laurence's text? Henry and his stage manager knew all about them—indeed, 'Bus. as known' was regarded as a professional secret. Surely they were for the benefit of those who were to follow?

Irving improvised in his last years—perhaps a talented covering-up of faulty memory; there was method in his madness. Beatrice Forbes-Robertson continues:

There were nights when the Governor was fluffy and nights when he was not, and while he was glad to be prompted on his 'off' nights, woe betide the actor who prompted him when he was only making a pause for effect.

During the dream-trial scene in 'The Bells', the whole company was on the stage, Mr Tyars, an experienced member, being seated as the Judge immediately behind Irving. He used to recite the whole of the star's long soliloquy *sotto voce*, so that Irving could pick it up at any needed point. But he seemed to have been overdoing it, for one night when we were all in place and the curtain about to rise Loveday (the Stage Manager), clad as always in tails, white gloves, and a gibus hat on the back of his head, popped on to the stage waving his hands.

'Ladies and gentlemen, attention please everyone. The Governor is not to be prompted tonight. Is that clear? No one on any account is to prompt the Governor!'

What improvisation was about to take place on those fatally-remembered, snow-clad hills to the delight and astonishment of his fellow actors? Beatrice is no longer here to tell us; perhaps it was like one told to me by a ninety-year-old gentleman who saw the play two weeks before Irving's death:

'What I will never forget is the wolves.'
'Wolves?'
'At Daniel's farm.'
'Ah! You mean the dogs?'
'No. Wolves. I remember every word: "How the wolves howl at Daniel's farm—like me they are hungry, searching for prey." And then he howled. It makes my hair stand on end when I think of it.'

Did a fluff at a previous performance inspire that improvisation of genius?

There remain the performances, described in loving detail by Eric Jones-Evans, of those who came after, seeking to perpetuate the Governor's creation—H.B.'s correct in every detail, thanks to the copied text; Harvey's romantic, graceful but lacking the *'diable au corps'* which Craig ascribed to Irving and based on faulty memory. There are letters from the late Walter Fiztgerald, who played with Harvey in *The Bells* during the thirties in which he describes the perils of such undertakings—would there be applause at the first entrance of Mathias? (This religious playgoers' ritual has become religiously observed.) 'As Father William, I entered before Sir John [Martin Harvey]. As I slammed the door shut against the elements and paused for breath, the audience would unaccountably bestow on me the entrance round they were reserving for Sir John. Even unknown actors must be permitted to make the most of their opportunities.' Secondly, Fitzgerald describes the daily pattern of rehearsals in terms of dialogues between Harvey and his wife Nina de Silva.

Harvey: At this moment, I remember, the Governor picked up the coin, said 'Ha!' and dropped it.

de Silva: No. He picked up the coin, dropped it and then said 'Ha!'

Harvey: You are mistaken, my love; it was as I have said.

de Silva (bursting into tears): You do not love me any more because I have grown old and you therefore contradict me.

Harvey: I still love you and will do so for ever, nevertheless, he said 'Ha!' and dropped it.[8]

Such passionate devotion to detail gets us nowhere. When Edward Craig saw *The Bells* in 1968, at its London fiasco, he said to me: 'I wish to God you had never read Father's book! In the first act, you were so constrained by his description of the man that you were powerless; in the second, you had less to go upon and were better; in the third, you had nothing but yourself and we took off.'

For those to come striving to continue the great Shakespeare and Burbage–Garrick–Irving tradition—read this book; digest every detail; but do not copy what you admire—use it.

Notes

1 Gordon Craig, *Henry Irving.*
2 Playbill in possession of the writer.
3 *The Era*, 3 December 1871.
4 Laurence Irving, *Henry Irving.*
5 Edward Craig has the detailed mechanical plans.
6 *The Times*, 26 April 1967; *Daily Telegraph*, 25 January 1968.
7 Beatrice Forbes-Robertson, *Family Legend* printed for private circulation, 1973, by Butler & Tanner Ltd, Frome and London, copyright Sanchia Phillips, 1973.
8 Letters in possession of the writer.

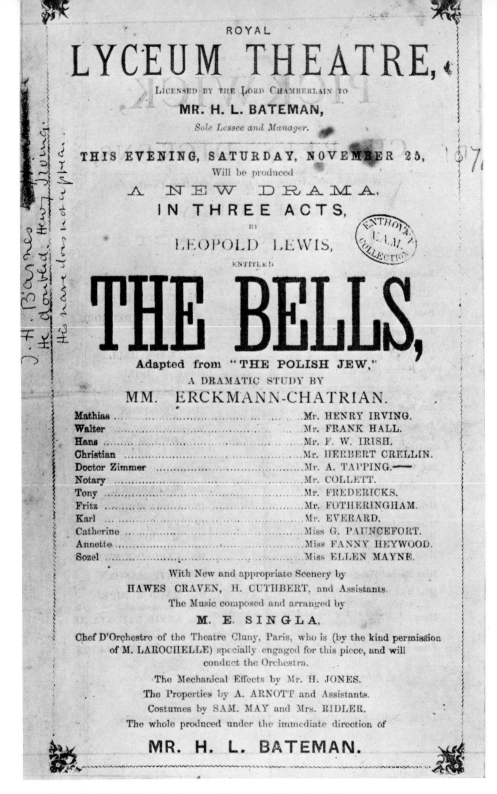

ROYAL
LYCEUM THEATRE,

LICENSED BY THE LORD CHAMBERLAIN TO

MR. H. L. BATEMAN,

Sole Lessee and Manager.

THIS EVENING, SATURDAY, NOVEMBER 25,

Will be produced

A NEW DRAMA,
IN THREE ACTS,

BY

LEOPOLD LEWIS,

ENTITLED

THE BELLS,

Adapted from "THE POLISH JEW,"

A DRAMATIC STUDY BY

MM. ERCKMANN-CHATRIAN.

Mathias	Mr. HENRY IRVING.
Walter	Mr. FRANK HALL.
Hans	Mr. F. W. IRISH.
Christian	Mr. HERBERT CRELLIN.
Doctor Zimmer	Mr. A. TAPPING.
Notary	Mr. COLLETT.
Tony	Mr. FREDERICKS.
Fritz	Mr. FOTHERINGHAM.
Karl	Mr. EVERARD.
Catherine	Miss G. PAUNCEFORT.
Annette	Miss FANNY HEYWOOD.
Sozel	Miss ELLEN MAYNE.

With New and appropriate Scenery by

HAWES CRAVEN, H. CUTHBERT, and Assistants.

The Music composed and arranged by

M. E. SINGLA,

Chef D'Orchestre of the Theatre Cluny, Paris, who is (by the kind permission
of M. LAROCHELLE) specially engaged for this piece, and will
conduct the Orchestra.

The Mechanical Effects by Mr. H. JONES.

The Properties by A. ARNOTT and Assistants.

Costumes by SAM. MAY and Mrs. RIDLER.

The whole produced under the immediate direction of

MR. H. L. BATEMAN.

Programme for *The Bells* at the Lyceum Theatre, 25 November 1871.

INTRODUCTION

The best of Victorian playmaking and acting share qualities with decorative and applied arts of that period. And like these arts, the stage inspires fascination. The products of these artists, at once so sturdy and so durable, intended for repeated, if not constant use, built to withstand travel and to impress in corners of Empire with the same force as at home, awe and reassure. But for all their apparent sturdiness, both decorative products and theatrical activities also impart a sense of instability, of excess and imbalance. Just as wood and metal, terracotta and stone are treated as fluids or fabrics teased into fantastic shapes, so in the Victorian theatre dialogue is stretched beyond the norms of daily conversation and human action pushed to the very limits, if not beyond the bounds, of acceptable causality.

The best products of the Victorian decorative artists are exciting, even alarming, for their utility and sturdiness are overlaid with exuberance, uncertainty and what we may often suspect is an excess of emotion. The heights of Victorian drama similarly unite surges of unruly energy, imbalance, and precarious emotional excess with a sturdy craftsmanship that quite unexpectedly assures stability, longevity and survival. Such qualities as these, the unruly, precarious and stable, belong to the enduring partnership between the actor Sir Henry Irving and *The Bells*, the play by Leopold Lewis in which Irving rose from the near obscurity of a character-comedian to the front rank of the English-speaking tragedians. From its first performance at London's Lyceum Theatre on 25 November 1871 until his death thirty-four years later, *The Bells* remained in Irving's repertoire and was performed throughout England and on eight successful tours of America. In its first season at the Lyceum, *The Bells* received 151 consecutive performances. In all, Irving performed its leading role above eight hundred times. *The Bells* was last performed by Irving but two nights before his death in October 1905.

Undeniably, plays other than *The Bells* received more performances in

Irving's lifetime, and perhaps plays other than *The Bells* serve as more typical examples of such a basic Victorian theatrical genre as melodrama. But no play better illustrates the last century's obsession with melodrama whose hero-villains are consumed by guilt and remorse, and no other drama quite so effectively demonstrates the intimate association between a leading actor of the British stage and the drama in which he appeared. Moreover, *The Bells* thoroughly deserves the recognition it received in its own time and again today as a remarkable psychological drama which compels its audiences to sympathise with a man guilty of a vicious murder, for although the audience soon come to recognise that the drama's protagonist Mathias is a criminal, they none the less cannot fully condemn him because Mathias's debilitating suffering forestalls recrimination. Better than any actor of his generation, Irving could enact the agonies of such suppurating guilt as Mathias's. *The Bells* was a vehicle suited to his ability, but other actors subsequently demonstrated convincingly that the play stands without Irving.

For many years we have known of Irving's association with *The Bells* and something of his onstage work in this play, but many assumptions about his performance in the role of Mathias have been erroneously based on the premise that the previously published text to *The Bells* is the text that Irving himself performed. Irving's own text to *The Bells* together with the musical score of this play make their appearance in this present edition. The text differs from other versions of the script both in respect to dialogue and in a wealth of detailed stage directions and indications of Irving's graphic stage business which illuminate many passages of speech. The score further enhances the play, for no melodrama is complete without the incidental music provided to accompany its action. Furthermore, Irving's text in this edition is explicated in moment-by-moment commentary by an actor who saw Irving's Mathias in one of the last performances that Sir Henry was to give in that role. With such a fund of new material at our disposal we are in a stronger position to reappraise Irving's greatness, and we are now able, should we wish, to bring Irving's own script before present-day audiences.

IRVING'S ASSOCIATION WITH *THE BELLS*

From the month in which he first appeared in this play, theatre audiences associated *The Bells* solely with Henry Irving. However, owing to his exceptional histrionic versatility, Irving's identity could never be tied to one particular play or role. And although other adaptations of a popular French psychological melodrama enacting the agonies of the guilt-haunted

2

Mathias were brought to the stage, no other version and no other actor attained anything resembling the success of Irving or *The Bells*. 'Colonel' Hezekiah L. Bateman, the lessee and manager of the Lyceum, had fortunately yielded to Irving's insistence that Bateman should produce the translation of the French play that Leopold Lewis had been hawking about to theatre managers, and Henry Irving shrewdly reworked Lewis's adaptation to assure himself of a vehicle which would exploit his talents as an exponent of the macabre. Not to be outdone, other actors competed with Irving in producing and playing the leading role of Mathias in less satisfactory adaptations of the play. But, lacking his acting ability and scripts so uniquely suited to their talents, they achieved little success in the part. Other versions of the play are largely forgotten.

Yet the weight of the partnership between actor and play was not wholly borne by Irving. Between his death and 1937 there were no fewer than nine 'replica' revivals of *The Bells* attempting to duplicate many details of the Lyceum production and performances—with the invariable exception that no one attempted imitations of Irving's voice. This extension beyond the 1870s and even beyond Irving's lifetime confirms the view that *The Bells* held powers of its own to draw audiences, that it satisfied theatrical tastes through numerous changes of theatrical fashion and answered emotional needs well into the age of Freud. Until the late 1930s the maxim persisted among touring actor-managers, 'When the treasury is low, Laddie, put on *The Bells*.' Today *The Bells* continues to be a landmark of Victorian drama and not merely to the reader and the scholar, for the play still finds audiences in the professional theatre. *The Bells* is also attempted by amateurs, although somewhat less frequently, because its taxing leading role and complex technicalities of staging overstretch amateur skills and resources.

Attempts to understand the singular success of *The Bells* must take into account several factors, none of which in itself explains why this play should have caught the public's attention. Certainly Irving's remarkable acting and his intense concentration on and attention to every element of the play's production account for *The Bells'* effect upon the first critics to view it. But those criticisms themselves, notably Clement Scott's review in *The Observer* on the day following, and John Oxenford's lengthier review in *The Times* (both reprinted later in the book) bestowed upon both *The Bells* and Irving the cachet of enthusaistic reviews in major publications and helpful publicity. Moreover, and this point cannot be underestimated, the script that Bateman and Irving acquired was a notably felicitous adaptation of *Le Juif Polonais*, a play which had been seen in Paris three years earlier. The lifting of the siege of Paris brought a fresh crop of French plays to the notice of London theatre managers and employment to their stables of translators. *Le Juif Polonais* was among this sudden yield, and the play's promise was soon turned to advantage. A mere thirteen days before the first night of *The Bells*, a rival English version was introduced to audiences at the Royal Alfred Theatre, Marylebone, under the title of *Paul Zegers; or, The Dream of Retribution*.

Le Juif Polonais by Emile Erckmann and Pierre Alexandre Chatrian, with a score by Etienne Singla, had been performed by Talien as Mathias in 1869 at the Théâtre Cluny. This melodrama depicts the final hours of an Alsatian burgomaster, outwardly an honest and genial leader of his village, but in his soul tormented by a guilty conscience that will not allow him to forget a murder committed fifteen years before to the very day. The Erckmann–Chatrian original and its first English adaptation by Frank C. Burnand only gradually reveal the burgomaster's festering guilt. It is not until the final act, as the burgomaster dreams that he is being tried before a high court and there, under the hypnotic power of the court-appointed mesmerist, compelled to re-enact the murder of the Polish Jew, whom he also robbed, that the audience is wholly certain of the burgo-master's villainy. *The Bells* differs in the particular that the guilt of Mathias is explicit by the end of the first act. His crime is visibly recalled in the 'vision scene' which closes the act, and this difference between a suggestion of guilt and the certainty that the burgomaster is concealing his guilt is an element which reached into the unconscious fears of Victorian audiences.

It is something of a current cliché and therefore near-exaggeration to state that the Victorian middle classes were individually and collectively troubled by guilt. Nevertheless, we increasingly recognise idealised and generalised public attitudes toward 'morality', a nineteenth-century euphemism for sexual behaviour and marital regularity that fell within socially acceptable norms. The Victorians publicly enthused over morality. On the subjects of marital and sexual irregularities they were less vocal. Often these were unmentioned as too disturbing or unpleasant to discuss. But the repeated exhortations to virtue speak loudly to the continuing existence of vice or extramarital liaisons, and there is ample evidence that in the 1870s as throughout the century, virtue in public masked vice in private. Therefore, a drama with a hero such as Mathias, who publicly lives a praiseworthy and blameless life but whose secret life is

4

one of criminal acts followed by guilty fear and torment eventually ended through confession and punishment, held out to its audiences the promise of emotional relief. *The Bells* offered to theatre audiences the opportunity to share vicariously the experience of criminal action, guilt, fear of discovery, and eventual retribution. *The Bells* may have dramatised a crime far greater than theatregoers were likely to have committed, but their guilt and repressed fear could well have been on a scale proportionate to Mathias's. In sharing emotions which touched on their own unconscious fears, first activating and then assuaging them, the audience gained a temporary but pleasurable respite from these fears. In this light it is significant that Henry Irving also enjoyed success in the roles of Macbeth and of Sir Edward Mortimer in a revival of Colman's *The Iron Chest*, another remorseful hero-villain who attempts and fails to conceal a vicious crime and who suffers appallingly from guilt.

The success of *The Bells* spawned its imitators and detractors. J. Redding Ware's *The Polish Jew; or, The Sledge Bells* made its debut at the Grecian Theatre on 4 March 1872, and another version, S. Emery's *The Polish Jew*, began its life on the 18th of the same month at the Theatre Royal, Bradford. *The Bells* also was travestied in a burlesque that began its touring life at the Theatre Royal, Norwich, on 13 March 1883, a year that found Irving in a national tour of *The Bells* and other Lyceum plays. As materially relevant to the popularity of *The Bells* were the replica productions of this play which followed from 1906 and are noted elsewhere in this volume. But even in Sir Henry's lifetime, music-hall audiences were entertained by Bransby Williams, 'The Irving of the Halls', who, in 1896, was presenting a popular feature programme of impersonations entitled 'Famous Actors and their Roles' which included vivid impersonations of Sir Herbert Beerbohm-Tree as Svengali in Trilby and of Irving as Mathias in 'The Dream Scene' from *The Bells*. In 1914 he changed the title to 'The Stagedoor Keeper' and included many more actors and music-hall artistes, but still retained Sir Henry in his most famous play.

LEOPOLD LEWIS

Irving's adaptor of *The Bells*, Leopold David Lewis, was not prepared for the play's reception or for Irving's exclusive rise to fame and prosperity. A solicitor by training, Lewis inclined toward journalism and at one time, with the caricaturist Captain Alfred Thompson, co-edited the satirical journal *The Mask*. *The Bells* was Lewis's first of two plays and only success. The best account of Lewis on the first night of *The Bells* is given by George R. Sims, later a prolific writer of melodramas and musical

comedies, but in 1871 a twenty-four-year-old journalist and popular balla-
deer soon to be known for such poems as 'The Workhouse, Christmas
Day' and 'Billy's Rose'. As Sims recalled in a retrospective column for the
Evening News:

> On the evening of the 25th November, 1871, as I was going Gatti-wards for
> a cup of coffee and a game of dominoes, I saw coming through the swing doors
> of a public house a gentleman wearing, among other things a pair of long red
> whiskers and a red woollen comforter. He greeted me in a husky voice. He
> had a very bad cold and had been taking hot rum and water for it. The gentle-
> man was a solicitor of Bohemian habits, who combined law with literature
> and both with hot rum, for which he had a weakness, and his name was Leopold
> Lewis.
>
> 'Hullo, my boy!' said Lewis, as he recognised me in the glimmering gaslight
> of a misty November evening. 'Papa Bateman is putting up a play of mine at
> the Lyceum, and I've got to see it. I don't fancy the play much—it's a toss-
> up how the audience will take it—but I think Irving's going to be good in it.'
>
> There were plenty of stalls vacant at the Lyceum, and the author and I sat
> in two of them. It was a long bill. There was a first farce, then *The Bells* with
> Irving as Mathias, and then an adaptation of Pickwick by James Albery in which
> Irving appeared as the jaunty Jingle, in order to give the audience some comic
> relief after the stress of 'The Polish Jew'.
>
> The first part of *The Bells* was not very enthusiastically received, but the
> audience was undoubtedly held by the big scene. In the stalls there was a general
> agreement that Henry Irving had fulfilled the promise of dramatic intensity
> which he had shown in his recitation of *The Dream of Eugene Aram*.
>
> The play left the first-nighters a little dazed. Old fashioned playgoers did
> not know what to make of it as a form of entertainment. But when the final
> curtain fell the audience, after a gasp or two, realised that they had witnessed
> the most masterly piece of tragic acting that the British stage had seen for many
> a long day, and there was a storm of cheers. Then, still pale, still haggard,
> still haunted, as it were, by the terror he had so perfectly counterfeited, the
> actor came forward with the sort of smile that did not destroy the character
> of the Burgomaster or dispel the illusion of the stage.
>
> The professional humorists parodied *The Bells* in the comic papers, and there
> were several burlesques of the play. I remember one atrocity produced in the
> provinces which was called *The Bells-Bellesqued and the Polish Jew Polished
> Off; or, Mathias, the Muffin, the Mystery, the Maiden, and the Masher.*
>
> Imitators of Henry Irving, his voice, his gait, and his gestures, were stock
> items in the programme of drawing room entertainments. In burlesques and
> extravaganzas comic actors got themselves up as doubles of the new tragedian
> and as I glance back to that far-off first night I remember that it was on that
> occasion that I saw the first appearance upon any stage of Mr. J. H. Barnes.

He played 'the double' of the poor conscience-stricken Burgomaster.

Poor Leopold Lewis never recovered from the success of *The Bells*. Henry Irving did everything possible for him and was generous in the extreme, but he became a man with a grievance. He believed that his adaptation of *The Bells* and not Irving's performance had made the fortune of the Lyceum. Eventually he fell upon evil days. He was found late one night seriously ill somewhere in Gray's Inn Road. He was taken to the Royal Free Hospital and there he died in February, 1890.[1]

ERIC JONES-EVANS

On Saturday 4 February 1905, a bare eight months before Sir Henry Irving's death in Bradford, a seven-year-old boy, already a playgoer from the age of four, was taken by his theatre-loving parents for the third time that week to the Grand Theatre, Boscombe, now a district of Bournemouth. These parents, the Rev. and Mrs John Llewellyn Jones-Evans, themselves both confirmed 'Irvingites' as Sir Henry's adoring fans called themselves, had determined that their son Eric should see some of the classic fare of the Lyceum repertoire: Tennyson's *Becket*, Charles Reade's *The Lyons Mail*, an adaptation of *The Courier of Lyons*, and *The Bells*, preceded by Conan Doyle's *Waterloo*. The effects of this experience were deep and ineradicable. Young Eric re-enacted Mathias's trial nightly in his bedroom, his face illuminated by the green light from a torch fitted with changeable coloured lenses that had been in his Christmas stocking. In 1906, Irving's elder son Henry Brodribb Irving undertook the first replica revival of *The Bells*. This production Eric saw at the Queen's Theatre, London, in 1909. Again, in 1917, at the Savoy Theatre he saw 'Harry' in his father's famous role of the haunted Burgomaster. This time he was able to speak at length with the actor about the original business introduced by Sir Henry when he first produced the play in 1871. Subsequently he saw many other replica productions of this drama. In later years as a professional actor, Eric Jones-Evans was eventually to perform every one of the male roles in this drama.

Professional acting was a vocation Eric Jones-Evans was to share with another career. In 1916 he began medical training at St Thomas's Hospital in Lambeth and qualified as a physician in time to be commissioned to serve as a Naval Medical Officer aboard ship in the First World War. It was while a medical student that he entered the professional theatre. A theatrical company touring the George R. Sims and Robert Buchanan drama *The Trumpet Call* lacked an actor, and Jones-Evans, to the derision of his fellow students, agreed to perform a role he had all but memorised through almost too frequent attendance at local playhouses. His first success was sufficient to induce him to return to the stage when the war ended and, concealing his medical training from his theatrical associates, he joined a first-class, change-nightly, touring repertory company owned by the actor-manager John Soden and his wife Kate Randolph.

Concealment, this time of his theatrical vocation, was again obligatory when Dr Jones-Evans decided to marry, for he feared that his wife-to-be would regard an actor's life with distaste. However, his guilty secret came out and, far from the reproofs and condemnation he anticipated, his wife fully approved of and encouraged him in his acting career. Thereafter, as Dr Jones-Evans, he maintained a medical practice in Fawley near Southampton and, closing his surgery on matinée days, performed regularly at the Grand Theatre in Southampton. In 1928, Dr Jones-Evans formed his own company which he maintained until the outbreak of the Second World War. For this company he wrote and appeared in a number of his own melodramas, chiefly adaptations of the novels of Dickens and George Eliot, and maintained close connections with other actor-managers, notably Sir John Martin-Harvey, Fred Terry, and Bransby Williams. These associations incidentally led to Dr Jones-Evans amassing a considerable collection of Edwardian playscripts, theatrical memorabilia and posters, much of which is deposited with the Russell-Cotes Art Gallery and Museum in Bournemouth.

More significant from the standpoint of this volume, Dr Jones-Evans, now in his eighties, enjoys the gift of keen observation and a memory which accurately recalls his first experience of seeing Henry Irving in *The Bells* and equally precise recollections of the many replica productions he saw between 1909 and 1934. His total recall and willingness to contribute these memories afford moment-by-moment commentary on Irving's own script, thus providing insight into Irving's mature stage business and into acting technique too subtle and private to have been included in either Lyceum prompt script or the published text.

It has been my responsibility as editor to verify Dr Jones-Evans' memories and assertions. I have been sceptical of each claim until from the evidence of playbills, programmes, newscuttings, and other printed sources, I have been able to confirm that his memories of persons, dates, places and activities are in all particulars correct. On the question of his memories of Irving's stage business, I have attempted to be equally stringent. The notes which Dr Jones-Evans appended to the text of *The Bells* (in addition to the comments of other contemporary observers of Irving,

8

and to my own sparse comments), were taken from many hours of tape-recorded conversations with him in which I cross-questioned him to be confident beyond doubt that in each instance the memory evoked was of Henry Irving and not one of the many replica productions he had seen or indeed ones in which he had performed or staged. In some instances, where a practice of staging originating with Irving continues through several replica productions (such as the stove door's hingeing and interior lighting in Act II), I have welcomed from Dr Jones-Evans a note which not only offers a view of Irving's meticulous care but which shows the vigour and tenacity of stage tradition. Each meeting with him has brought with it the fascination and excitement of being instructed in late Victorian and Edwardian theatre-practice, a reason among many others I have thoroughly enjoyed and benefited from my association with Eric Jones-Evans. He is a major fund of anecdote, lore, and theatrical knowledge, a living link with the age of Irving, priceless and unique.

TEXTS OF *THE BELLS*

The nature of this script to *The Bells* and its provenance require explanation and interpretation. There are, in all, three distinct texts of *The Bells*. The earliest of these is a version in longhand manuscript deposited with the Lord Chamberlain's Inspector of Plays in November 1871, and granted a licence in the same month. It is now held by the Manuscript Department of the British Library (ADD. Ms. 53102K). Very likely this version is close to the translation and adaptation Leopold Lewis had hawked about to various theatre managers earlier in the year. Eric Jones-Evans, in recalling his backstage conversation with H. B. Irving in 1917, remembers Irving claiming that Lewis had previously submitted his translation of *Le Juif Polonais* to managers at the Adelphi, Surrey, and Britannia and to Bateman at the Lyceum. All including Bateman had rejected it. Laurence Irving, in his biography of his grandfather, states that Lewis then approached Henry Irving, who recognised in this script a vehicle for his own style of acting and in subsequent negotiations with Bateman made it a condition of his employment that Bateman would produce *The Bells* with Irving as Mathias. Laurence Irving further claims that Irving himself bought the rights to *The Bells* from Lewis.[2]

The truth of these claims cannot be verified, nor can one determine with accuracy when Lewis received the script to *Le Juif Polonais* and made his translation. It is equally uncertain when Lewis offered his work to the several theatre managers, was rejected by them and thereafter approached Irving. Nor is it known when Irving declared his interest and when, in

9

the autumn of 1871, *The Bells* was put into rehearsal. What is probable is that Irving, intent on appearing in *The Bells*, persuaded Bateman to secure the rights to Lewis's translation in the form of a lease rather than outright purchase and that Irving and Lewis collaborated to produce the version close to the text which Irving used in November. This version, submitted to the Lord Chamberlain's Reader and licensed, was altered shortly before the first performance by the removal of Catherine from the 'vision scene' that ends the first act. It is also probable, but not certain, that the opening moments of the third act were altered at this time, for such an emendation was made to the text in its early days. Somewhat later in the run, Mathias's gift to Annette was changed from an Alsatian hat to a gold necklace. Other changes of dialogue, stage directions and business, and music cues were made as Irving developed his own role and recognised further possibilities for his supporting casts.

The second extant version of *The Bells* is the text issued by the dramatic publishers Samuel French Limited, and subsequently by two lesser London publishers. The history of the published version is, to say the least, clouded and vexed by discrepant accounts. However, it would appear that in April or May of 1872, when *The Bells* was nearing the end of its first season's run of 151 consecutive performances, H. L. Bateman leased the publishing rights for a five-year period to French's, the earliest published copy bearing the warning:

> *Notice*
>
> The exclusive rights to represent this Drama, or grant permission for its representation, in the United Kingdom, the Channel Islands, and the Isle of Man, are vested in Mr. H. L. Bateman of the Royal Lyceum Theatre, London, from the 3rd of July last [i.e. 1872], to the 29th June, 1877, after which date such rights revert to the Author.

In 1877 the rights therefore reverted to Lewis, and Lewis, according to Bram Stoker, resold the rights to French's only to have them subsequently repurchased by Irving:

> Colonel Bateman originally leased the rights of the play from the author Leopold Lewis. Finally, at a time of stress—sadly frequent in those days with poor old Lewis—he sold them to Samuel French from whom Irving finally purchased them. Notwithstanding this double purchase Irving used, after the death of Lewis, to allow his widow a weekly sum whenever he was playing—playing not merely *The Bells* but anything else—up to the time of his death.[3]

The Samuel French text has been identified by its publishers as likely to be the early Lyceum text simplified for professional touring and amateur performances. The stage entrances and locations of furnishing and properties have been printed in accordance with conventional practice, the Lyceum settings notwithstanding. In each Act the settings are reversed (as if described from the auditorium) from the disposition of scenery, furnishings, and movements described in Irving's script. Moreover, the music cues bear only a notional resemblance to those necessary for Singla's Lyceum score. In addition to the script published by French's, new translations of *Le Juif Polonais* entitled *The Bells*, but distinctly dissimilar to the Lyceum play, were published by Maclaren & Co. at some date before Irving's death, and by Hugo's Language Institute in 1922. It is not in any way remarkable, therefore, that Irving made no objection to continued publishing of variations of *The Bells*. His own version with its score were his exclusive property.

The third version of *The Bells* is the one published in this volume. It is Sir Henry Irving's personal script, typed with pencilled addenda and emendations which passed at his death to his son Henry Brodribb ('H.B.' or 'Harry') Irving, the tattered script remaining in his possession until his death in 1919. The script was presented by Laurence Irving to Marius Goring. It differs in numerous particulars from both the manuscript version and published texts. The differences between Irving's text and the two other versions are found in the considerably augmented stage directions and, to a somewhat lesser degree, in passages of dialogue. Irving's text alone retains its appropriate incidental music. As an example of differences, we may look to the moment in Act II when Mathias's prospective son-in-law Christian first voices professional interest in the Jew's murder. In the Samuel French edition, this passage is as follows:

CHRIS. You know, Burgomaster, I do not bring much.

MATH. You bring courage and good conduct—I will take care of the rest; and now let us talk of other matters. You are late today. I suppose you were busy. Annette waited for you, and was obliged to go without you.

(*He goes up and sits by stove in armchair, opens stove door, takes up tongs and arranges fire.*)

CHRIS. (*unbuckling his sword and sitting in chair*) Ah, it was a very curious business that detained me. Would you believe it, Burgomaster, I was reading old depositions from five o'clock till ten. The hours flew by, but the more I read, the more I wished to read.

MATH. And what was the subject of the depositions?

CHRIS. They were about the case of the Polish Jew who was murdered on the Bridge of Vechem fifteen years ago.

MATH. (*dropping the tongs*) Ah!

CHRIS. Father Walter told me the story the night before last. It seems to me very remarkable that nothing was ever discovered.

MATH. No doubt—no doubt.

In the Irving text, the stage business of the actors is made more explicit, and the dialogue somewhat more relaxed before Christian injects the note of tension:

CHRIS. Well, you know, Burgomaster, I don't bring much.

MATH. (*Hand on* CHRIS.'s *shoulder*) You bring courage and good conduct. (*Playfully slapping his face*) I'll take.care of the rest. And now let's talk of other things.

(CHRIS. *up stage, takes off sword belt, puts it with cap and gloves on chair up L.* MATH. *goes to chair R. of stove, takes paper from table and walks down reading to armchair R. of stove.*)

You were late to-day. Annette waited for you for some time, but finding you did not come——

CHRIS. (*Interrupting*) Ah, yes, it was a very strange circumstance that detained me. (*Bumps chair from L. places it in front of stove and sits.* MATHIAS *has sat in armchair R. of stove and has opened it to feed it with coke.*) Would you believe it, Burgomaster, I've been reading over old depositions from five o'clock till ten—the time passed, but the more I read, the more I wanted to read.

MATH. (*laying handkerchief on his knee*) Old depositions—to what did they refer?

CHRIS. (*leaning forward, arms on knees, hands clasped, not looking at* MATHIAS) Why to that case of the Polish Jew (MATHIAS *is leaning down picking up coke with tongs, drops coke and looks up. His face is illuminated with the red light from the fire*) who was murdered on the bridge of Vechem. Father Walter and Hans told me the story the day before yesterday, and I've never been able to get it out of my head. (MATHIAS *drops tongs*) It is to me perfectly astounding that nothing was ever discovered.

MATH. (*Looking at* CHRIS. *with alarm*) No doubt, no doubt.

Irving's version of *The Bells* has been exactly transcribed, but the limited descriptions of setting have been supplemented with further scene descriptions and drawings of floorplans indicating the disposition of scenery and properties at the rise of curtain for Acts I, II and the three scenes of Act III. Dr Jones-Evans provides further notes on lighting, scenery, and the operation of scene changes. The groupings of characters for the 'Dream Scene' and final scene of Mathias's death are specified in Irving's script. Music cues in the script, with few noted exceptions, correspond to Singla's Lyceum score, and this score is discussed at greater length in Nigel

Gardner's introduction to the music. As there were eleven major revivals and subsequent tours of *The Bells* between its original production in 1871 and Irving's relinquishing of the Lyceum management in 1902, and as thereafter *The Bells* was almost permanently in Irving's repertoire, it is highly doubtful that this script is the one Irving first performed. More probably it is Irving's text successively modified as the actor developed his role of Mathias.

The overture and incidental music for the drama was specially composed and arranged by M. Etienne Singla, *Chef d'orchestre* of the Théâtre Cluny, Paris, for *Le Juif Polonais*, and used in the premiere performance of *The Bells* at the Lyceum on 25 November 1871. Bateman brought Singla from Paris to the Lyceum to arrange his score for this performance, and according to the programme Singla conducted at the first performance. It is uncertain whether Singla's entire score was used on this occasion. However, in the course of time, Irving deleted many of the musical themes introducing the principal performers and thereby tautened and heightened various dramatic sequences. The musical directors associated with Henry Irving at the Lyceum were Mallandaine, Meredith Ball, Hamilton Clarke and, for the farewell tour of 1905, Sydney Ffoulkes, who later became the conductor to the Julia Neilson–Fred Terry Company. The score and band-parts passed at Sir Henry Irving's death to H. B. Irving to be used in both the 1909 and 1917 revivals. They were also used by Henry Baynton and Sir John Martin-Harvey in their own productions of the play. When Sir John died in 1944, Lady Martin-Harvey presented the band-parts to Dr Jones-Evans.

HENRY IRVING AS A PERFORMER

Finally, there are the recollections and reflections that Eric Jones-Evans offers of Henry Irving's acting: descriptions, interpretations, and assessments that are realised and confirmed in the pairing of Irving's personal script with Jones-Evans's memoir and notes to the script. What emerges from these comments is a view of Henry Irving, by no means the first to be offered in this vein, as an actor meticulous in his preparation taking infinite pains to achieve the emotional, intellectual, and theatrical possibilities inherent in his text. Calculation, revision, scrupulous attention to scenic effects, stage lighting, hand properties and their manipulation, emotive music, but above all to the minute and intimate details of acting were characteristic of Irving. However, to state that Irving's acting was calculated and dependent upon planned movements, planned gestures, and carefully tuned nuances of intonation is not to claim that

13

Irving lacked spontaneity. Quite the contrary. If Irving's work in *The Bells* is a reliable guide to his performances in other plays, we can then recognise how diligent preparation freed his emotional energy to flow from inner levels, on occasion from the unconscious itself. Dr Jones-Evans's testimony confirms the impression of others that acting loosed the daemonic in him, that Irving's face and eyes, his voice, and at times his body expressed raw feeling uncensored by intellect or constrictions of dialogue.

The calculated element of Irving's work most often mentioned in conversations and correspondence by Dr Jones-Evans was the actor's concern with timing. Repeatedly he describes Irving playing a waiting game with his audiences, pausing, hesitating, pursuing such a moment of stage business as slowly peering into his wine glass for a speck of floating cork or deliberating upon finding a coin from the Jew's money belt, thereby allowing his audiences to read his mind, to share his character's thoughts and even his thought processes before fitting words to these thoughts. But again, each of these drawn-out moments contains a further element, the abruptly terrifying lifting of a mental barrier to expose a depth of authentic panic or horror or revulsion beyond the capacity of other actors to express. Such revelations pleasurably shocked and titillated audiences who only moments before had felt confident of their understanding of the character on stage before them. Here were new, alarming, unfathomable depths.

If we are to grasp why theatregoers were awed by Irving's playing, why precise details of Irving's acting have to this day rooted themselves in the memory of Eric Jones-Evans, we must recognise that Irving was both a consummate technician who through meticulous preparation and close study of his audiences' responses sought and compelled the spectators' undivided attention and, as well, an uncompromisingly honest artist capable of releasing genuine emotion into his work at each performance. In neither technique nor display of emotion was there excess or extravagance. Irving enacted what was essential, what was clear, and because it was essential and clear, Irving's art was unforgettable.

NOTES TO INTRODUCTION

1. George R. Sims, *Glances Back* (London, 1917), pp. 53–8.
2. Laurence Irving, *Henry Irving, the Actor and his World* (London, 1951), pp. 172–3.
3. Bram Stoker, *Personal Reminiscences of Henry Irving*, vol. 1 (London, 1906).

14

Music cover for Etienne Singla's 'Lauterbach' played in Act II of *Le Juif Polonais* at the Théâtre Cluny in 1869. The illustration depicts the dancing in the 'contract scene', with Talien as Mathias sitting amongst the waltzing dancers.

DON'T SEE THE NAME OF MR. LEOPOLD LEWIS ON THE COUNCIL!

(*Above left*) cartoon of Leopold Lewis, translator and adaptor of *The Bells*, by Alfred Bryan for *The Entr'acte*, 30 June 1883; (*above right*) Clement Scott, critic for *The Observer*, whose review of *The Bells* helped to establish Irving's reputation and generated popular interest in Lewis's play; (*below left*) Bram Stoker, Henry Irving's business and acting manager, biographer of Irving and author of the novel *Dracula* and (*below right*) caricature of Hawes Craven, Irving's scenic artist, by Alfred Bryan for *The Entr'acte*, undated.

WITH IRVING AND *THE BELLS*

Were it not for my parents' consuming interest in the theatre, I should never have seen Sir Henry Irving perform the role of Mathias in *The Bells*. Nor, without them, would I have spent so many happy hours in the stalls and dress-circle seats of theatres in London and the provinces.

It was to the delightful, elegant and unspoilt seaside town of Bournemouth that my mother and father retired at the turn of the century, and enjoyed regular weekly visits to the Theatre Royal, the Winter Gardens, and the Grand Theatre, Boscombe. My father—the late Rev. John Llewellyn Jones-Evans, M.A., who, prior to his retirement, had been the vicar of Sydling St Nicholas in Dorset—and my mother, a talented musician and painter, were theatre enthusiasts and avid followers of Sir Henry Irving. As for his adorable colleague and partner, Miss Ellen Terry—her skill as an actress, in their opinion, was unrivalled. And their critical admiration embraced most of the supporting members of the Lyceum Company.

This devotion to Irving and his Lyceum regime undoubtedly had a pre-natal effect upon me. My father had seen the actor so many times as Mathias that he knew the entire play by heart—stage business, character grouping, scene sets and furnishings, lighting and music—the lot. And so, at a very early age, did I. For 'George' (the nickname I had given my father, from his fondness for golfing with George Robey—Father adored being called by it) used to quote many of the lines to me, and sing snatches of the incidental music which I loved—the 'Lauterbach' in particular. Furthermore, my mother and father had spent a glorious honeymoon in London visiting the Lyceum Theatre every night for a month. No wonder I was born with an ardent desire to tread the boards as an actor!

From this preamble, it will be realised that my parents were unusally far-seeing and regarded the theatre as a necessity in a civilised world. They also believed—as did Irving—that God was in the Theatre: a creed which—at that period—was not universally accepted by the Church. In-

17

deed, a number of distinguished prelates likened the doors of a playhouse to the gates of Hell!

I am, therefore, doubly grateful to my forebears for having such advanced views, and for training my visual-auditory senses to such a high degree. In fact, my upbringing was equivalent to that of a child born to theatrical parents. So strongly determined were they that I should share their enjoyment of every type of entertainment that, from the age of four, I was taken once a week to matinée performances at either the Theatre Royal, Bournemouth, or the Grand at Boscombe. By the time I was seven I had become a seasoned playgoer, having seen most of the Gilbert and Sullivan light operas, countless touring melodramas, a vast number of West End musical comedies, and a succession of the famous autumnal Drury Lane society dramas written by Cecil Raleigh and Henry Hamilton.

When the posters announcing that Sir Henry Irving and his Company would be visiting the Grand Theatre for three nights and a Saturday matinée on their farewell tour my father was one of the first patrons to visit the box-office and reserve his usual seats in the third row of the stalls. They were for the evening performance of Tennyson's *Becket* on Thursday 2 February 1905; *The Lyons Mail* by Charles Reade, with Irving in the dual roles of Lesurques and Dubosc (Friday evening, 3 February); and on Saturday evening, 4 February, *The Bells*, preceded by Sir A. Conan Doyle's one-act play *Waterloo*, in which Sir Henry played the veteran Corporal Gregory Brewster. The matinée performance was *The Merchant of Venice* which, since I had to rest before the late night ahead, I did not see. But those four performances were destined to give me the final impetus to become a provincial touring actor.

After a couple of hours' rest and an early tea, which I was almost too excited to eat, I rapidly donned my dark-grey Norfolk suit, Eton collar and tie, in readiness to accompany my more sumptuously dressed parents. 'George' wore his customary clerical evening attire, while my mother, looking very attractive, was arrayed in what I suppose would be described as 'the latest from Paris'. Then, according to the custom of those far-off days, a hired horse-drawn brougham arrived to take us from our home to the theatre.

The house was crammed to capacity—every seat having been booked weeks before the opening date. Even standing room was no longer available in either the pit, the dress-circle, or the gallery.

The regular theatre orchestra, composed of twelve to fourteen instrumentalists, occupied its usual position in the musicians' pit. But on this occasion the conductor was Mr Sydney Ffoulkes—a brilliant director and composer whom Irving had engaged for the farewell tour. Many years later, when he became musical director for the Julia Neilson–Fred Terry Company, I used to meet him in the cosy dress-circle bar of the Grand Theatre, Southampton. There, over a couple of sparkling gin and tonics, we would discuss at length that final tour of 1905 which terminated in the death of Sir Henry Irving after playing Becket at the Theatre Royal, Bradford, on the night of 13 October. Incidentally, Sydney Ffoulkes composed the incidental music for *Henry* of *Navarre* and *The Wooing of Catherine Parr*—two romantic dramas by William Devereux—which, when produced and played by Fred Terry and his charming wife, Julia Neilson, proved popular successors to their *Sweet Nell of Old Drury* and *The Scarlet Pimpernel*.

While the orchestra played Singla's overture to *The Bells*, we eagerly scanned our programmes and commented on the cast in whispers. My father took my programme and, with a pencil, marked the old-time actors from the Lyceum Theatre (which Sir Henry no longer owned) who were members of the touring company (asterisked below). They totalled eight in number! The rest were all newcomers. Overleaf is a copy of the programme, which includes the cast of *Waterloo*.

As my memories are so closely connected with Sir Henry's own version of the play and the stage business he invented for it, I think it would be more practical to bring them forth as sequential notes to the amended text, and this practice I propose to follow. Yet there are some recollections which are so strong, so deeply ingrained, that they stand apart from the script as if I were turning the pages of a scenic-artist's sketch-book. For instance, when the curtain rose on Act I the audience immediately became aware of the cosy, genial warmth and homeliness radiating from the old inn-parlour with its quaint furniture and panelled walls. It was only when we saw through the large window at the back, its red curtains not yet drawn, the fast-falling snow in the gathering dusk of that Christmas Eve, and heard the moan of the rising wind that we suddenly felt a strange premonition that all was not well—that some fearful tragedy was about to occur.

A little later on in that act, I recall the spine-chilling sensation I experienced as Father Walter—the village carrier, factotum and gossip—related the dramatic story of the Jewish seed merchant who had mysteriously disappeared after visiting the inn during a violent snowstorm on Christmas

WATERLOO
(1815–1881)
By Sir Arthur Conan Doyle

Corporal Gregory Brewster (aged 86, a Waterloo Veteran)	Henry Irving
Sergeant Archie McDonald, R.A.	Mr Lionel Belmore*
Colonel James Midwinter (Royal Scots Guards)	Mr Vincent Sternroyd
Nora Brewster (the Corporal's Grandniece)	Miss Maud Fealy

Scene—Brewster's Lodgings

TO BE FOLLOWED BY

THE BELLS
Adapted by Leopold Lewis from 'The Polish Jew' by
Erckmann Chatrian

Mathias ..	Henry Irving	President of the Court ..	Mr F. Tyars*
Christian	Mr H. B. Stanford	Clerk of the Court ..	Mr William Lugg*
Walter..	Mr Charles Dodsworth*	Mesmerist ..	Mr J. Archer*
Hans	Mr James Hearn*		
Dr. Zimmer ..	Mr Mark Paton*	Catherine	Miss Grace Hampton
Notary ..	Mr Leslie Palmer	Sozel	Miss Mary Foster
Fritz	Mr Tom Reynolds*	Annette ..	Miss May Holland

SYNOPSIS OF SCENERY

Alsace 1833

ACT I.   Scene—The Burgomaster's Inn
ACT II.   Scene—The Burgomaster's Parlour
ACT III. Scene—The Burgomaster's Bedroom
—The Dream

PROGRAMME OF MUSIC

Medley—'Rank and File'	Meredith Ball	Czardas	Keler Bela
'Marche Russe' ..	Luigini	'Les Cosaques' ..	Ellenberg
Overture—'The Bells' .. Singla		Hungarian Dances ..	Hamilton Clarke

Eve fifteen years previously. He was about to reach the climax of his narrative when a violent gust of wind, followed by a crash of breaking glass, was heard in the adjoining kitchen. It transpired that the serving-maid Sozel, had negligently left a window open, and the storm had smashed several panes of glass.

When the general consternation had subsided, Father Walter continued his story of the missing Polish Jew: 'The next morning,' he said, 'the Jew's horse was found dead under the bridge of Vechem, and a hundred yards further on the green cloak and fur cap, deeply stained with blood. As to what became of the Jew himself to this day has never been discovered.' What a grand part for an actor! I should know, for I have often played it.

The entrance of Sir Henry Irving as Mathias, a little later on, is another vivid memory. And, once again, Father Walter and Hans, the forester, had created the build-up for it with the technical expertise of their stage business and dialogue. The conversation of the two old cronies has turned to Mathias who, at the time of the Polish Jew's disappearance, had been a comparatively poor man, and heavily in debt.

'Now,' said Hans, 'he is one of the richest men in the village, and the Burgomaster. He certainly was born under a lucky star.'

'Well, he deserves all the success he has achieved', was Father Walter's reply.

During that brief duologue, exciting but unobtrusive atmospheric incidental music (technically known as a 'Hurry') was being played in the orchestra. Before it reached its zenith, a shadowy figure was dimly seen striding past the window through the snow. The inn door was flung open, and there, amid the whirling snowflakes, stood Mathias—riding-whip in hand—his long fur coat and otter-skin cap covered with snow.

''Tis I!' he cried, slamming the door to behind him, to shut out the icy wind. ''Tis I! At last! At last!' Then with both arms extended to embrace his wife and daughter, his pale, handsome face with its clean-cut features glistening with the melting snow, he patiently waited for the tumultuous applause to subside.

But it didn't. For a full half-minute (my father timed it), the clapping, the shouts of 'Bravo', and the thunder of stamping feet in the gallery continued. It was a fantastic reception—the second he had received that night. For in the curtain-raiser 'Waterloo', in which Sir Henry had played the veteran Corporal Gregory Brewster of the 3rd Guards, the audience had already extended a vociferous welcome to England's greatest actor.

And here's another memory. Towards the end of the first act, Mathias was about to drink a glass of Alsatian wine when the subject of 'the missing Polish Jew' was mentioned. I shall never forget how he paused in the act of raising the glass to his lips, and peering into it to conceal his consternation, pretended to remove a fragment of cork from the wine with his little finger.

'So, you were talking about that, were you?' he murmured, wiping his finger on the table-cloth. Wipe, wipe, wipe. 'You were talking about that, eh?' It was at that moment that he heard, and so did we, the far-off jingling of sleigh-bells. 'Bells!' he whispered. 'Sleigh-bells on the road!' The sense of fear and horror conveyed by Irving in that whisper still has the power to make me shudder.

The memories now are coming thick and fast. The one I am about to recall is the finale of the first act. Hans and Walter have departed on their homeward journey. Mathias is left alone. The ghostly jangling of the bells comes nearer, now accompanied by a menacing *andante mysterioso* from the orchestra. Running to the window, Mathias tears back the curtains and looks out. 'No one on the road,' he mutters. 'No one! What is this jangling in my ears? What is tonight?' As he draws the curtains again, the grandfather clock in the corner chimes the hour of ten. His terror increases.

'Ah!' he cries, ''tis the very hour! The very night.' He staggers down to the chair right of the table. 'I feel a darkness coming over me; a giddiness seizes me!' To prevent himself from falling, he catches hold of the chair back. 'Shall I call for help? No, no, courage, Mathias. Courage! The Jew is dead—dead! Ha, ha, ha! Dead!' He collapses into the chair, burying his face in his hands. As he does so, the back of the scene rises and sinks and, through a gauze, which gives the effect of mist, we see the snow-covered country with the Bridge of Vechem and the frozen rivulet. In the distance a lime-kiln is burning. Through the falling snow, the crouching figure of a man dressed in a peasant's brown blouse, the hood of which conceals his face, is seen carrying an axe. He is following a horse-drawn sleigh in which a Polish Jew is travelling. At intervals, scudding snow-clouds obscure the ghostly pale-blue light emitted by the wintry moon. The jingling of the bells grows louder.

Mathias, his fingers in his ears, rises and slowly walks to down stage right. 'It's nothing!' he murmurs to himself. 'The wind and the cold have overcome me!' Pausing momentarily, he turns and walks up stage centre.

'It's nothing, nothing, *nothing.*' Suddenly looking up, he sees the vision of himself stalking his victim through the snow. With a shriek of terror he falls to the floor centre stage, as the curtain rapidly descends. And that was the ending of Act I.

There were further highlights, I recall, in Act II of this splendid drama. These were the counting of Annette's dowry; the fascinating scene with Christian—the Quartermaster of gendarmes—when Mathias discusses with him the problematical fate of the Polish Jew; the signing of the marriage contract, followed by Annette singing the traditional Alsatian bridal song; and the gay abandon with which the guests and villagers danced the 'Lauterbach' as a finale to the Act.

As for the third act with its vivid and terrifying 'Dream scene'—the stage business created by Irving was so intricate that only by audio-visual means can an approximately accurate reproduction of it be obtained. To make this possible, Mr Michael Hall—Director of the professional film-unit in the Department of Drama at Bristol University—kindly invited me to re-enact on film some of the more complicated scenes from the play for preservation in the archives of the Department. It gave me great pleasure to comply with his request, and two colour films are now available. (See the Bibliography.)

The recollections of my first visit to *The Bells* with Sir Henry Irving in the role of Mathias still further impress upon me the exceptional quality of his stage business. So much of the effect lay in his sense of timing. Muscle control enhanced his power of facial expression to such a degree that, without uttering a word, the audience would know what he was thinking. But he seldom relied upon a succession of well-tried effects. There was always something fresh and unexpected; some added element that had not been planned or rehearsed with which he electrified the house. And that was especially so in *The Bells*. His dropping of the fire-tongs in the second act was a planned effect, but there was at the same instant something in his mind so raw and horrific and apparently spontaneous. And in the famous 'Dream scene' in which he re-enacted the murder of the Polish Jew, the bestial blood-lust in his face and eyes, as he struck the fatal blow went far beyond acting and mere effect. At these moments Irving was a man possessed by a devil from the pit of Hell.

What I have recorded here are just a few of the vivid memories I retain after seeing Irving that night at the Grand Theatre, Boscombe, and they are wholly unforgettable. Strange to relate, they become even fresher and clearer as I grow older. And further recollections will be found in the notes that follow Henry Irving's own text of *The Bells*. His version incorporates all the amendments made during rehearsal, and describes in detail the original stage business devised by him. It also contains comprehensive lighting and scene plots for the play. (Incidentally, stage lighting at that period was produced by argand gas-jets in the floats and overhead battens combined with perch limes fitted with coloured glass mediums that could be changed at the discretion of the operator. This system proved ideal for lighting the beautiful scenery painted by Hawes Craven, William Cuthbert and Walter Hahn, the resident scenic artists at the Lyceum Theatre.) My recollections are assisted but not confused with recollections of the many replica productions I saw afterwards. These were replicas in the sense that they followed Henry Irving's business as well as the actor-managers could recall it, and they attempted to use the familiar costumes and settings. But just as each production failed to catch Irving's unique qualities, each of those many Mathiases gave something of their own to the role. I hope that in my time I did.

After the death of Sir Henry Irving, I saw most of the revivals—in both London and the provinces—of this splendid drama which had brought fame and fortune to our first actor-knight. Sir Henry's elder son, H.B. ('Harry' to his friends) who, physically, facially, vocally and temperamentally was a perfect replica of his distinguished father, had valiantly essayed the role of Mathias in Chicago, on 18 December 1906, when making his first and only professional visit to the U.S.A. His performance was politely received, but created no particular stir. This was mainly due to the fact that, though the name of Irving was revered by playgoers throughout America, 'H.B.' was quite unknown to them as an actor, and had not yet won his spurs.

On returning to England in the spring of 1907, he added *The Bells* to a repertoire of his father's older plays, and toured the provinces. His reception was most encouraging, and the critical reviews of his portrayal of Mathias were excellent. Two years later he became lessee and manager of the Queen's Theatre in Shaftesbury Avenue; and on 22 September 1909 made his London debut as the haunted Burgomaster. Both the production and his performance were greeted with enthusiastic applause from the audience, and approval from the critics.

As a special birthday treat, I was taken by my mother and father to see two performances of this revival. The entire presentation and H.B.'s portrayal of Mathias were exact replicas of what I had seen at the Grand Theatre, Boscombe, on that never-to-be-forgotten Saturday night in 1905.

24

One technical change, however, drew my attention. Instead of the 'Sink and rise' for the vision at the close of Act I, the set divided laterally. This method was employed ever after, being so much simpler and eliminating the necessity for cutting 'slots' in the stage floor.

On 19 May 1917, at the Savoy Theatre, London, I again saw H.B. in a revival of this haunting play which, for me, has been a life-long obsession. On this occasion, he had engaged for his Christian—the Quartermaster of Gendarmes—a young Shakespearian actor named Henry Baynton, about whom I shall have more to say later. Little thinking it would be the last time I should see H. B. Irving in *The Bells*, I decided to indulge in a theatrical orgy by paying six consecutive visits to my favourite psychological drama of the macabre. And very rewarding it was. Apart from seeing at each performance an exact facsimile of the late Sir Henry, I was able to have long and fascinating talks about the play with H.B. in his dressing-room while he was making-up.

In the spring of 1918 (when I was a Surgeon-Sublieutenant in the R.N.V.R.) H.B.'s health was on the decline. Never physically robust, the stresses and strains of actor-management and touring proved too much for him. On 20 October 1919, after a distressing and debilitating illness, a truly gifted and well-loved actor, who was also an erudite criminological author, passed peacefully away.

Now for Mr Henry Baynton. This well-graced actor, who had toured with Oscar Asche and Sir Frank Benson's No. 3 Shakespearian Company before joining H. B. Irving at the Savoy, took up the reins of actor-management when the run of *The Bells* terminated in 1917. Forming his own company, he toured the provinces with a large repertoire of Shakespearian and romantic plays. The venture proving a success, he embarked on a further series of tours, adding the conscience-stricken Burgomaster Mathias to his list of characters. For this production of *The Bells*, he presented the drama in two acts, by playing Act II—without making any textual alterations—as Scene 2 of Act 1. His answer to my inquiry as to why he had done so was a smiling, 'I don't really know. I just wanted to be different from "H.B." and Sir Henry.' Which, to my mind, seemed a logically sound reply.

In the provinces, where Shakespearian and romantic costume dramas were still popular, Henry Baynton's portrayal of Mathias was received with acclamation. This encouraged him to enter into negotiations with Robert Courtneidge in 1924 to present *The Bells*, with a condensed version of *The Comedy of Errors* as a curtain-raiser, for a short season at the

25

Savoy Theatre in London. The critics, inevitably comparing Baynton to Sir Henry and H.B., were not exactly encouraging, and the following review from the *Daily Telegraph* for me expresses the problems that bedevilled Baynton's production, as I recall them, and the still greater complexities that confronted all of us who followed in Sir Henry's footsteps.

... It is just over fifty years since the piece was first done at the Lyceum, and there, as the event proved, laid the foundation stone of Henry Irving's fortunes and reputation. After his death it reverted, by right of heredity, to his son 'H.B.', whose performance as Mathias, if hardly rising to the same level as that of his distinguished father, well merited the praise bestowed upon it. 'The Bells' is, of course, a one-part play, and must stand or fall by the success—or failure— of the leading actor. By temperament, appearance, and personality Irving was fitted, as nearly as anyone could hope to be, to a role in which the elements of psychology, tragic expression, and pathos are so largely blended. In attempting to follow in his footsteps Mr. Henry Baynton commits himself to a task of undoubted difficulty. That he emerges from the ordeal with flying colours can hardly be said. In the earlier scenes his acting yesterday was marred by an affected manner of speaking, while the feeling of mystery with which Irving enveloped himself as with a cloak, never quite reached the point of absolute conviction. There is a marked difference also in the fashion the long soliloquy in the second scene of the first act was handled by him and his famous predecessor, the first contenting himself with speaking the lines, while these were changed by the latter into a vehicle for the display of an extraordinarily tense and forceful piece of acting wherein the inmost emotions of the man were laid bare.

There remains the scene of the trial. In that Mathias, although only in a dream, passes through all the stages of agonised despair. Mr. Baynton's stage management at this point is much less effective than was Irving's, whose example he might advantageously have followed. At the Savoy the principal character takes his place in the middle of the stage, with two very obvious spotlights trained upon him. Those who remember the Lyceum setting will recall the profound feeling of eeriness produced by the comparative gloom which shrouded the members of the Court, placed well up stage. It was as if the voices of the judge and hypnotist issued from the recesses of a dark cavern. The effect was electrical. Mr. Baynton has, doubtless, been handicapped by the exigencies of a production designed for touring purposes, and probably any shortcomings on his part will be viewed with complaisance by the public to which he makes his appeal. It may at least be said in his favour that at the point indicated he played with a measured hysterical force that fairly carried his listeners away, and which secured for him an exceedingly cordial reception on the final fall of the curtains.

Having seen Henry Baynton as Mathias many times in the provinces, and also at the Savoy in 1924, I would describe his performance as follows:

Though uneven, it contained many moments of grandeur and inspired acting. But it would have been wiser had he waited half a decade before essaying the role. Frankly, he was too young and immature as an actor to undertake with complete success so complex a character as Mathias. He also lacked the power of portraying the terror and soul-destroying agony of mind that a convincing delineation of the conscience-stricken Burgomaster requires. In short—he was not an Irving. Nevertheless—and this is important—he seldom failed to enthral his audiences, whether in the provinces or the metropolis. And they, in turn, extended their devotion to a Shakespearian and romantic actor, who was dedicated to his art.

We now come to Bransby Williams, who—billed as 'The Irving of the Halls'—became a star on the night of 26 August 1896 when, at the London Music Hall, Shoreditch, he presented a life-like impression of Sir Henry Irving as Mathias in the 'Dream scene' from *The Bells*. That impersonation remained in his repertoire during his career as a star of stage (legitimate and variety), screen, radio and television. And that exalted position in the hierarchy of the theatrical world he retained until his death at the age of ninety-one on 3 December 1961. For over thirty years we were close friends, and I had the honour of appearing with him in stage plays and on television. His impression of Irving in the role of Mathias I had seen many times—the first being at the Tivoli in the Strand with my father, when I was still a stage-struck lad but old enough to be an ardent Irvingite.

It was as a touring actor, when he was serving his apprenticeship to the art he loved so well, that Bransby Williams played Mathias in the Leopold Lewis version of *The Bells*. That was before my time, and so I never saw him in the stage play. But I did see him in the first television version of the drama produced by Michael Barry for the B.B.C. on Tuesday 14 March 1950. For an actor of eighty years of age, it was a superb performance. Four years later, knowing my vocal versatility, he insisted on my playing the Public Prosecutor, the President of the Court, and the Mesmerist, to his Mathias in a television presentation of the 'Dream scene' on the stage of the Shepherd's Bush Empire by the B.B.C. on 24 April 1954. For me, that was a night of nights—a thrilling experience.

On 9 February 1933, at the Empire Theatre, Southampton, I first saw Sir John Martin-Harvey play Mathias. Harvey (he received the accolade in 1921) had been a member of Sir Henry Irving's company at the Lyceum for fourteen years, and had therefore many opportunities of seeing the actor-knight as Mathias. Like H. B. Irving, he used Singla's original music score adapted for the Lyceum pit orchestra. He even obtained some of

27

the furniture and properties used in the first Lyceum production. But he did not use Irving's script for his presentation of the play. Nor did we see the familiar vision at the end of Act 1. Instead, Sir John reverted to the original Erckmann–Chatrian finale in which a Polish Jew, seeking shelter from the blinding snowstorm, enters the inn and calls for wine. Unbuckling a money-belt, he throws it upon the table, and Mathias— terror-stricken by the strange coincidence—collapses and falls to the floor with a piercing cry.

Sir John's reason for altering the ending was the enormous expense— owing to post-war increases in freight charges—of transporting the extra scenery, property horse and sleigh needed for the vision. Nevertheless, by his powerful acting he succeeded in making the finale very effective. Incidentally, after Sir John's death on 14 May 1944, the Jew's money-belt was presented to me by Lady Martin-Harvey, and can be seen at the Russell-Cotes Art Gallery, Bournemouth, in the Irving collection. During 1933 and 1934, I saw Sir John play Mathias half a dozen times. His performances were moving, sensitive, and full of fire: but he was never so vivid, so detailed, so willing to bare his innermost soul to the audience as Irving was.

In 1916 I saw the late Edward Dunstan play Mathias several times at Birmingham, and a very sound characterisation he gave. Dunstan was a talented, provincial actor-manager of the old school, who—following in Sir Frank Benson's footsteps—ran a Shakespearian repertory company. As an added box-office attraction, he also presented such popular dramas as *Richelieu, David Garrick, Sydney Carton* and *The Bells*. Whenever I went to see him, he was playing to capacity houses—indisputable proof of his popularity. Other touring provincial actor-managers whom I saw as Mathias in the far-off days of my youth were Allan Wilkie, Ellerslie Pyne, and Edwin Beverley. Every one of them gave convincing and, at certain moments, inspiring interpretations of an exceedingly complex and emotive character.

Now for my own performances in *The Bells*. When in 1919 I was demobbed from the Navy, I joined the old-established, first-class, change-nightly, touring fit-up company owned by John Soden (an excellent Mathias) and his wife Kate Randolph, both of whom played the 'star' leads. For them I eventually acted every male role in *The Bells* except the Burgomaster. That glorious opportunity came in 1928 when I formed my own company, and our reception in the famous drama of crime and remorse was both enthusiastic and encouraging. As for me, to assume the role of Mathias was the fulfilment of an actor's dream. When I revived it in 1929 and 1933, we again played to capacity houses and the treasury rejoiced exceedingly.

Owing to the outbreak of the Second World War in the autumn of 1939, I was obliged to disband my company. But I continued, at intervals, to tour my one-man, quick-change Dickensian Entertainment, in which I included the 'Dream scene' from *The Bells* to give audiences an idea of what Henry Irving did, and what he stood for in the theatre of his time. Mathias proved a spine-chilling rival to Fagin's last night in the condemned cell at Newgate. And that's saying something!

THE BELLS

Portrait of Irving by Cyrus Cuneo depicting Mathias's entrance in Act I. The artist has reversed the hingeing of the door. Irving entered on its left.

COSTUME PLOT

CATHERINE. Middle-aged and greying. Pleasant, homely features. Wears an Alsatian dress of good quality befitting the wife of a well-to-do innkeeper and Burgomaster.

HANS. A forest-keeper. Getting on in years, with grizzled hair and sideboards. A cheerful, florid face that betokens a fondness for good living. He wears a square-cut undercoat of dark green, a double-breasted beige waistcoat with vertical green stripes, green velveteen knee-breeches and spatterdashes. On his head is a round fur cap with ear-flaps tied under his chin. This and his heavy drab coloured caped overcoat are covered with snow. A woollen muffler conceals the points of his upturned shirt collar showing above a black cravat tied in a bow. He carries a long-barrelled flintlock gun, and a game bag is slung over his shoulder.

SOZEL. A serving maid at the inn. She is a peasant girl aged about twenty. Wears a rather shabby, though picturesque, Alsatian dress with an apron tucked up on one side.

ANNETTE. A pretty blonde girl of nineteen to twenty years of age. She wears a dainty Alsatian frock (black corsage laced up in front). In Act II she wears a cloak and the traditional Alsatian hat.

FATHER WALTER. The village gossip and factotum. Middle-aged, with dark hair greying and going thin on top. His clean-shaven, jovial face with its well-defined features is somewhat pale. Though of the peasant type, he is better educated than Hans, and has a keen sense of the dramatic. This is most noticeable when he relates the story of the missing Polish Jew in Act I. Beneath a heavy grey overcoat he wears a dark blue square-cut coat and knee-breeches,

Watercolour studies of Alsatian costumes by William Margetson, R.I., made for Irving about 1895 when he w

a double-breasted red waistcoat with gilt buttons, black woollen stockings and buckled shoes. His coat and wide-brimmed black hat are covered with snow.

CHRISTIAN. Aged about thirty, tall, well built and handsome. He wears the regulation uniform of a Quartermaster of Gendarmes with a heavy blue cloak, gauntlets, sword-belt and sabre. He is clean-shaven.

MATHIAS. Middle-aged, with greying hair and a pale face. He wears a snuff-coloured square-cut coat and knee-breeches; a waistcoat with vertical brown stripes on a beige background; black stockings and buckled shoes. This portion of Irving's costume for Mathias is owned and exhibited by the London Museum. For Act I he dons a long fur coat, otter-skin cap, scarlet muffler, gaiters and spurs. (See note for Irving's Act I entrance.)

DOCTOR ZIMMER. An elderly pedantic type of man, with greying hair and spectacles. He wears a professional suit of black, and carries a malacca cane and a valise containing drugs and instruments.

NOTARY. Middle-aged. Wears a beige square-cut coat, flowered waistcoat, black breeches and buckled shoes.

PRESIDENT OF THE COURT. Judge's robe of scarlet and round black cap.

JUDGES. Same as President.

CLERK OF COURT. Black gown and white tabs.

BARRISTERS. Black gowns and white tabs.

MESMERIST. Dressed in black—similar to the Doctor.

GUESTS AND VILLAGERS. Wear a variety of colourful Alsatian costumes. In Act II the girls carry posies of flowers, and everyone wears a wedding favour (white or blue rosette) pinned on their coat or corsage.

ntemplating refurbishing the wardrobe for *The Bells*.

THE SET FOR ACT I

The scene depicts the shadowy, candle-lit interior of an Alsatian inn. The walls are panelled in dark oak and adorned on each side with three stags' heads. At the back, right of centre, a door, opening on-stage, leads to the village street. Left of centre is a large window, the dark red curtains of which are not yet drawn. To the left of this stands a charcoal stove, with an angled flue-pipe passing through the left wall of the room. Below the stove is a heavy oblong table (set up and down) with chairs placed left, right, and above it. On the table is a lighted candle, and, on a wooden tray, a covered tobacco-jar and a pewter pot containing pipe-spills. Stretched between the flue-pipe and the left wall is a line from which kitchen towels and washing-up cloths are suspended.

Up-stage right—in the angle formed by two walls—stands a tall grandfather clock. Below this, a door (half open) leads to the kitchen. Set against the right wall, down stage, is a large dresser. On its shelves are pewter plates, serving-dishes, and various items of domestic crockery. In front of this, right of centre, is a circular table with a lighted candle and a small mirror on it. A small wooden stool stands on its left. Below the table is a spinning-wheel with a stool set above it. Above the whirring of the wheel, the wintry gale is heard; and, through the window, rapidly falling snowflakes can be seen. These fall from a snow-cradle suspended in the flies above the outside door and window.

N.B. The oak-panelling in all the sets is dark.

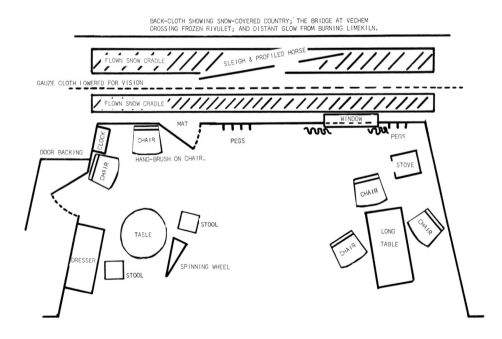

ACT I

MUSIC (Overture). Curtain up end of overture.

SCENE: Christmas Eve, interior of a village inn in Alsace—the residence of the Burgomaster. Back of scene, with door and window. Doors R. and L. 3 stags' heads on each flat R. and L. Pegs for hats, R. and L. Stove up L. with pipe to go through L. flat with line and towels. Lighted candle on small table R. Lighted candle and wood matches and tobacco on tray, L. table.

(MUSIC 1 for curtain)

LIGHTS thus: 1st down to $\frac{1}{4}$
            2nd Out } *Borders*
Foots blue $\frac{3}{4}$ down, blue, up gradually at beginning of scene to full.

(CATHERINE discovered at Spinning wheel. HANS passes window, and enters door R.F. He is covered with snow and carries a long gun and game bag across his shoulder.)

HANS. *(At door, taking off his hat and shaking the snow off)* More snow, Madame Mathias, more snow! *(Places gun by L.F.)*

    Stop MUSIC 1.

CATH. *(Seated R.C.)* Still in the village, Hans?

HANS. Yes, on Christmas Eve, one may be forgiven some small indulgences. *(Laughs)* *(Taking off his coat, hanging it on pegs)*

CATH. You know your sack of flour is ready for you at the Mill?

HANS. Oh, yes, but I am not in a hurry. *(Puts coat up.)* Father Walter will take charge of that for me in his cart. *(His back to stove.)*

CATH. Father Walter? Is Father Walter here? I thought he had gone long ago.

HANS. No, he is still at the Golden Fleece, enjoying his bottle *(laughs)* as I came along I saw his cart outside the grocer's, with the coffee, cinnamon, and sugar, all covered with snow (*laughs*). (*Sits R. of table L.*) He certainly is a jolly old fellow, and fond of good wine too (*laughs*). (*Filling pipe and laughs.*)[1] Ah, well, I don't blame him—Oh, you may be sure we will go home together.

CATH. And you do not fear being upset?

HANS. Upset, what does it matter? As I said just now, on Christmas Eve, one may be forgiven such slight indulgence you know—(*laughs*). And now, one glass of wine, Madame, and I'm off. (*Sits at R. of table.*)

CATH. I will lend you a lanthorn when you go.

HANS. Thank you, Thank you. (*Filling pipe*)

CATH. (*Calling, without moving from her seat*) Sozel! Sozel!

SOZEL. (*From within R.*) Yes, Madame.

CATH. Some wine for Hans.

SOZEL. (*As before*) Yes, Madame.

HANS. That's the sort, considering the festive character of seasons like this, one really must take something stronger than melted snow (*laughs*).

CATH. Yes, but take care! Our white wine is very strong.

HANS. Oh, never fear! (*Sits R. of table L. Lights pipe.*)

(*Enter* SOZEL, *with wine and two glasses from D.R. After placing them on the table, she waits up stage by stove.*)

But where is your Burgomaster? How is it he is not to be seen? Is he ill?

CATH. He went to Ribeauville five days ago.

SOZEL. Here's the wine, Master Hans.

HANS. (*Seated R. of table L.*) Good! (*Pours out a glass and drinks with gusto.*) Ah! And so the Burgomaster is at Ribeauville?

CATH. Yes, we expect him back this evening, but what is the use depending on men when once they are away.

HANS. Ah, you may rest certain that his cousin Both would not let him return in a hurry. That's the sort of life I should like to lead, travelling constantly through the Wine country, tasting samples and making purchases, instead of being doomed to look after nothing better than a wood. Here's your health, Madame Mathias! (*Drinks.*)

CATH. (*Turns towards him, bowing.*) Thank you.

36

HANS. I wager now that the Burgomaster has gone to Ribeauville to buy the wine for the wedding?

CATH. (*Laughing*) Not at all improbable. (*All laugh.*) (*Seeing* SOZEL *up L.C.*) Why, what are you standing there for, Sozel, have you nothing to do? Go and light the small lanthorn, Hans will take it with him. There, go along. It is very strange that servants always will listen to what takes place. (*Exit* SOZEL, *she runs off D.R. without reply.*)

HANS. Oh, I shouldn't have mentioned it, only a few minutes ago when I was at the Golden Fleece, it was talked about publicly that the pretty Annette, the daughter of the Burgomaster, and Christian, the Quarter-master of Gendarmes, were going to be married. (*Seated R. of table*) I could scarcely believe my ears! Christian is certainly a brave man—and an honest man—and a handsome man—I do not wish to maintain anything to the contrary. Indeed, our village is rather distinguished in that respect—Ahem, but he has nothing but his pay to live upon, whilst, Annette is the richest match in the village.

CATH. Do you think, Hans, that money ought to be the sole consideration?

HANS. No, no, certainly not—on the contrary—only I thought that the Burgomaster—

CATH. Well, you have been mistaken. Mathias did not even ask— What have you? He said at once, 'Let Annette give her free consent and I give mine.'

HANS. And did she give her free consent?

CATH. Yes, she loves Christian. And, as we have no other thought but the happiness of our child, we do not look for rich suitors.

HANS. Oh well, if the Burgomaster consents and you consent, and Annette consents, why I suppose I can't refuse my consent either. Only, I may make this observation I think Christian a very lucky dog, and I wish I was in his place.

(*Enter* ANNETTE D.R. *Runs to window and looks out, then turns to and addresses Hans.*)

ANNETTE. Good evening, Hans.

HANS. (*Turning around*) Ah, it is you—good evening, good evening, we were just talking about you.

ANNETTE. (C.) About me?

HANS. Yes—(*Looking at* ANNETTE *with sly significance and admiringly*) Oh, oh, how smiling you look, and how prettily dressed! One would almost think that you were going to a wedding.

ANNETTE. Ah, you are always joking.

HANS. No, no, I am not joking—I say what I think, that's all, those pretty shoes, that pretty dress, were not put on for a tough middle-aged forester, like myself. It's been all arranged for another, and I happen to know who that particular 'other' happens to be. He, he he!

ANNETTE. How can you talk such nonsense! (*Takes R. and down a little.*)

HANS. Oh, no, it's not nonsense.

> (FATHER WALTER *now crosses the window and appears at door in F. and putting his head in—Annette turns expectantly to look at him.*)

WALTER. (*Laughing and coming in*) Ha! She turned her head! It is not he! It is not he! (*Takes brush from chair and brushes snow off his boots, hat, coat, etc. on mat.*)
(*Hans rises, goes to his coat and sits L. of table L.*)

ANNETTE. Who, Father Walter?

WALTER. Ha, ha, ha, that's right. Up to the last minute, she'll pretend that she knows nothing.

ANNETTE. (*Simply*) I don't understand what you mean. (*Over at table R. back to audience*)

WALTER & HANS. (*Laughingly*) Oh, no, don't you, don't you, Oh, don't you, don't you?

CATH. Oh, you are a couple of old fools.

WALTER. Ah well, you are not such an old fool as you look are you, Hans?

HANS. (*Rather grumpy*) No! And you don't look such an old fool as you are! Do you, Walter? (*Both laugh.*)

> (*Enter* SOZEL *R. with a lighted lanthorn, which she places on table R. and exits D.R.*)

WALTER. What's that lanthorn for?

HANS. Why, to act as a light to the cart.

ANNETTE. (*Rises, goes to table.*) You can go by moonlight.

> *Annette opens the lanthorn and extinguishes the candle.* (*Then brings stool, sits L. of Catherine. Both Walter and Hans laugh.*)

WALTER. Yes, yes, certainly, we will go by the light of the moon. (*Hans has poured out wine.*) Here's to the health of Christian and Annette!

HANS. Yes, here's the health together of Christian and Annette.

(*WIND*)

(*They touch glasses and drink, Hans taking a long time to drink the contents of his glass.*)

WALTER. (*Seriously*) And now, listen, Annette, as I entered I saw Christian returning with two Gendarmes and I am sure that in a quarter of an hour—(*sits head of table L.*)

(*WIND off L.*)

ANNETTE. Listen! (*Goes to window.*)

CATH. The wind is rising.[2] I hope that Mathias is not now on the road.

ANNETTE. No, no, it is Christian.

(CHRISTIAN *passes the window and enters door F. covered with snow*—ANNETTE *runs to him, opening the door.*)

CHRIS. Good evening, all! (*Stands on mat, brushes off snow, etc.*) Good evening, Annette (*Kisses her hand.*) (*She shuts door.*)

ANNETTE. Where have you come from, Christian?

CHRIS. From the Hovald.

(ANNETTE *exits door R.*)

From the Hovald! What a snowstorm! I have seen many in Auvergne, and on the Pyrenees, but never anything like this before. (*By this time he has brushed off the snow, hangs his cap, gloves and cloak on chair behind stove and advances to stove and warms his hands.*)

(*Re-enter* ANNETTE *with wine, etc. goes over to stove.*)

WALTER. (*As* ANNETTE *places a jug of wine on the stove*) There, look at that! What care she takes of him! (*Lighting his pipe and smoking, laughing to* HANS) It would not be for us she would fetch the sugar and cinnamon and warm the wine.

CHRIS. (*To* ANNETTE, *laughing*) Do not allow me, Annette, to be crushed by the satire of Father Walter who knows how to defy the wind and the snow by the side of a good fire. I should like to see the figure he would present if he had been five hours in the snow on the Hovald as I have been.

ALL. Five hours in the snow, Christian? Your duties must be terribly severe.

CHRIS. How can it be helped? At two o'clock we received information that the Smugglers had passed the river the previous night with tobacco and gun-powder, so we were bound to be off at once. (*Crosses to* CATH. *and bends over her talking.*)

(ANNETTE *now pours some hot wine into a glass and advances with* CHRISTIAN.)

ANNETTE. (*L.C.*) Drink this, Christian, it will warm you.

CHRIS. (*Standing C.*) Thank you, Annette. (*Takes glass, looks at her tenderly and drinks.*) Ah, that's good!

WALTER. The Quarter-master is not difficult to please.

HANS. No, not very. (*Patting* WALTER *on the back.*)

CATH. Never mind him, Christian, never mind him—you are fortunate to have come this early. (*Goes to window.*)

(*WIND L.H.*)

(CHRISTIAN *goes to table L. to make cigarette.*)

Listen to the wind! I hope that Mathias will have stopped for shelter somewhere on the road—(*to* HANS *and* WALTER) I was right, you see, in advising you to go—you would now have been safely at home.

HANS. (*Laughing*) Annette was the cause of our stopping—Why did she blow out the lanthorn?

ANNETTE. (*By* CHRISTIAN) Oh, you were both glad enough to stop.

WALTER & HANS. (*Laugh*) Ha, Ha, Ha, ha.

CHRIS. (*C.*) Your winters are terribly severe here! (*Advances*)

WALTER. Oh, not every year, Quarter-master.

CHRIS. No!

WALTER. We have not had a winter so severe as this for fifteen years.

CHRIS. Indeed.

HANS. No, I do not remember to have seen so much snow since what's called the 'Polish Jew's Winter'. In that year the Schalberg was covered in the first days of November, and the frost lasted till the end of March.

CHRIS. (*C.*) And for that reason it is called 'The Polish Jew's Winter?'

WALTER. No, it is for another and more terrible reason that none of us will ever forget. Madame Mathias remembers it well, I'm sure.

CATH. You are right, Walter, you are right.

HANS. Had you been here at that time, Quarter-master, you might have won your cross.

(*WIND.*)

CHRIS. (*Interested*) Won my cross. How? How?

WALTER. (*At table, lighting his pipe*) I can tell you all about the affair from the beginning to the end since I saw it nearly all myself. (*Drinks.*)

CHRIS. (*Much interested*) Do.

(*Christian brings chair to L.C. and sits.* ANNETTE *C. by R. side of* CHRISTIAN.)

Let us hear all about it.

WALTER. (*After a slight pause*) Curiously enough it was this very day, just fifteen years ago.

CATH. & HANS. So it was, indeed.

CATH. This very night.

WALTER. I was seated at this very table—there was Mathias who sat there (*points R. of table*) and who had only bought his mill just six months before—there was old John Roebec, who sat there (*points L. of table*)—they used to call him the 'Little Shoe-maker'. (*Puffing out smoke*)

HANS. & CATH. Ay! Poor old John.

WALTER. And several others, who are now sleeping under the turf. Ah! We shall all go there some day, all, ay, ay, Happy are those who have nothing on their conscience, (ALL, Ay.) We were beginning a game of cards, when just as the old clock struck ten, the sound of sleigh bells was heard upon the road. A sleigh stopped before the door, and almost immediately afterwards a Polish Jew entered. He was a well made man and vigorous, between forty and fifty years of age—I fancy even now I can see him enter at that door (*points to door R.C., all turn and look*) with his green cloak and his fur cap, his large black beard and his great boots covered with bear-skin. He was a seed-merchant. As he entered, he said, 'Peace be with you.' Everybody turned round to look at him, as much as to say, 'Where has he come from?' 'What does he want?' Because, you must know, Quarter-master, that the Polish Jews who come to dispose of seed don't usually arrive in this province till the month of February. (CHRIS. Yes, yes, I know.) Mathias said to him, 'What can I do for you?' But the Jew, without replying, opened

41

his cloak, then unbuckled a girdle that he wore around his waist, threw it down upon the table, and all heard the ringing sound of the gold it contained. He then said, 'The snow is deep, the road difficult—put my horse in the stable; in one hour I shall continue my journey.' He then drank some wine without speaking to anyone, and sat like a man depressed, and who is anxious about his affairs. At eleven o'clock the night watchman came in. Everyone went his way, and the Jew was left alone.

> (*Loud gust of wind, L. Wood and glass crash, R.*)³ (CHRISTIAN *keeps his seat, the* OTHERS *start to their feet in alarm.*)

CATH. What has happened? I must go and see. (*Going R.*)

ANNETTE. Oh, no, you must not go.

CATH. Do not be alarmed—I will return immediately.

> (*Exit* CATHERINE *D.R. with candle from small table R.*)

CHRIS. But I do not see how I could have gained the cross in the affair? (*Brings chair nearer* WALTER)

WALTER. Stop a minute. (*They sit again.*) The next morning they found the Jew's horse dead under the bridge of Vechem, and a hundred yards further on the green cloak and the fur cap, deeply stained with blood. As to what became of the Jew himself to this day has never been discovered.

HANS. Everything that Walter has stated is strictly true. The Gendarmes came here the next morning, notwithstanding the snow; and in fact, it is since that dreadful time that the brigade has been established here.

CHRIS. But was no enquiry instituted?

HANS. Enquiry! I should think there was! (*Both laugh.*) It was the late Quarter-master Kelz who undertook the case,—how he travelled! What witnesses he badgered! What information and reports were written, and how the cloak and cap were analysed and examined by magistrates and doctors, but it all came to nothing. It all came to nothing.

CHRIS. But surely suspicion fell on someone.

HANS. Oh! Suspicion. (*Both laugh.*) The Gendarmes are never at a loss for suspicion in such cases, (WALTER. That's a dig at you, Quarter-master (*he laughs*)) but proofs are required. Now, about that time, you see, there were two brothers living in the village who had an old Bear with his ears all torn, two big dogs, and a Donkey, that they took about with them to the Fairs and made the dogs bait the bear. This brought them a good deal of money; and they lived a rollicking dissipated life. When the Jew disappeared, these brothers happened to be at Vechem, and suspicion fastened on them, and the report was, that they had caused the Jew to be eaten by the dogs and the bear, and that the animals only refrained from swallowing the cloak and cap because they had had enough already. The brothers were arrested, and it would have gone hard with the poor devils, if Mathias had not interested himself in their case, and they were discharged after being in prison fifteen months, and their animals had been slaughtered. That was the only suspicion they had in the case.

CHRIS. What you have told me greatly astonishes me. I have never heard a word of this before. (CHRISTIAN *arises, puts chair to table and crosses down L. and back*.) (ANNETTE *puts stool over R*.)

(*Enter* CATHERINE *door R*.)

HANS. It is all true, every word of it.

CATH. I was sure of it. Sozel had left the windows in the kitchen open, and now every pane of glass in them is broken. Oh, oh, oh, (*to Chris*.) Fritz is outside, he wishes to speak to you.

CHRIS. What, Fritz, the gendarme?

CATH. Yes; I asked him to come in, but he would not. It is upon some matter of duty.

CHRIS. Ah, good, I know what it is. (*Puts on his cap, gloves and cloak, and goes towards the door R*.)

ANNETTE. You will return Christian?

CHRIS. In a few minutes, Annette, in a few minutes. (*Kisses her hand*.)

Exit CHRISTIAN *D.R*.

WALTER. Ah, there goes a manly young fellow—gentle in character, I will admit, but not a man to trifle with rogues.

HANS. Yes, Mathias is fortunate to find so good a son-in-law; but everything has succeeded with Mathias for the last fifteen years. He was comparatively poor then, and now he is one of the richest men in the village, and the Burgomaster. He certainly was born under a lucky star.

WALTER. Well, he deserves all the success he has achieved.

MUSIC 2.[4]

(MATHIAS *passes the window*.)[5]

At last! At last!

43

(MATHIAS *enters,*[6] *takes off cap, throws it with whip R. and embraces* CATH.) *Stop* MUSIC 2.

'It is I!—It is I!'

MATH. It is I!—it is I! At last! At last!

CATH. At last!

MATH. At last! Heaven be praised! Burr! What a snowstorm! I was obliged to leave the carriage at Vechem. It will be brought over to-morrow. Ah, my darling. (*Embraces* ANNETTE.)

CATH. Let me help you. How good of you not to stop away. Do you know, we were getting quite anxious about you? (*Takes brush from chair and hands it to* MATHIAS, *who brushes snow from boots,*[7] *then throws it R.*)

MATH. So I thought, Catherine. (*Embracing her*) And that was the reason why I determined to reach home to-night. (*Embraces* ANNETTE *again and sees* WALTER.) Ah, Father Walter. (*Crosses and shakes hands with* WALTER.) And Hans. (*Gives hand to him.*) You'll have nice weather to go home in, won't you? (*They laugh.*)

(MATH *goes down to* C. *wiping neck with handkerchief and staring out as if impressed with what he has gone through with the mesmerist.*)[9]

You will have to get those things well dried.

CATH. Yes, dear! Sozel! (SOZEL. (*off*)—Yes, Madame?) Get your master's supper ready at once. (SOZEL. Yes, Madame) And tell Stephen to take his horse to the stable.

ANNETTE. (*Bringing down chair R. of table L. to C.*) We thought perhaps ...

MATH. (*Starting*) Ah, my darling. (*Embracing her.*)

ANNETTE. We thought perhaps your cousin Both had detained you.

MATH. Both! No, no. (*Sitting down in chair C.*) I'd finished my business yesterday morning, and I wanted to come away.

(*Annette has knelt on his L. and is about to unbuckle his boot—Cath. has picked up pair of shoes, with shoehorn and gives Annette the L. shoe.*)

Don't touch that, dear, it's nasty and wet. (*Unbuckles boot, and draws it off with other foot.*)[10] But Both would make me stop to see some performance in the town.

ANNETTE & CATH. A performance!

ANNETTE. A Punchinelle at Ribeauville?

This and all subsequent photographs of Henry Irving in *The Bells* are from a group of thirteen carte-de-visite-size photographs taken by the London Stereoscopic Company within a year of the opening of the play in November 1871. All were posed in the photographers' studio, not on the Lyceum stage.

44

MATH. (*Who has taken off L. boot and half the R. boot*) (*Sits up and places an arm around each Annette and Catherine*). No, no, it was not Punchinelle—it was a—Parisian—who did the most extraordinary tricks—he—he—sent people to sleep.

CATH. & ANNETTE. Sent people to sleep?

MATH. Yes, fast asleep, fast asleep.

CATH. Oh, he gave them something to drink, no doubt.

MATH. (*Still with arms around women*) No, he didn't do that, he simply looked at them,—and—made—made—some signs. (*Waves right hand about without withdrawing arms, the women both look at hand.*) and they went—fast asleep,—fast asleep. (*Takes hands away, and proceeds to put on R. shoe.*) It certainly was a strange performance. Well, if I hadn't seen it myself, I should never have believed it.

'It certainly was a strange performance. Well, If I hadn't seen it myself, I should never have believed it.'

HANS. (*Seated L. of table L.*) Ah, the Brigadier Stenger was telling me about it the other day.

MATH. (*Putting on R. shoe*) Ah, yes, Stenger, how is old Stenger?

HANS. He had seen the same thing at Saverne. This Parisian sends people to sleep (CATH. *and* ANNETTE *have left* MATHIAS *and gone up to table, listening to* HANS) and when they are asleep he makes them tell everything that weighs upon their conscience.[11]

(MATHIAS *has been buckling up. R. shoe and at the word 'conscience' he looks up in fear and slowly sits upright during which* HANS *is telling the others at table in pantomime how it is done*).[12]

MATH. Exactly, exactly. (*Recovering himself*) Annette. Annette.

ANNETTE. (*Turns and runs to him.*) Yes, father.

MATH. Look in the big pocket of my coat.

(*Enter* SOZEL *who comes down to get boots.*)

Ah, Sozel, how are you? Hang those boots and spurs in the harness room.

SOZEL Yes, Burgomaster.

(*Exits with boots R.*)

ANNETTE. What is it, Father? (*She has taken basket from coat hung up R. and has been excitedly undoing wrapper.*) What is it, Father?

MATH. Open the box, open the box. (*Still seated*)

45

ANNETTE. (*Takes necklace from box.*)[13] Oh, Father! Oh! How pretty—(*Runs down to mirror on table R.*) Is it for me? (*Trying it on*)

MATH. For you. Why, who else could it be for? (*Turns round at Walter and Hans.*) Not for Sozel, I fancy. (*They laugh.*)

ANNETTE. (*Turning round*) What will Christian say?

MATH. Say? Why you're the prettiest girl in the Province.

ANNETTE. (*Crossing to Math.*) Thank you, dear father. (*Arms round him.*) How good you are.

MUSIC 3

(MATH. *pauses, kisses her hands, looks up to her furtively and takes both of her hands, brings her round in front of him and then pulls her slowly on to his R. knee caressing her.*)

MATH. (*Seriously*) That's my wedding present, Annette. I want you to wear it on your marriage day and preserve it forever. Do you think now that in fifteen or twenty years you will remember that your father gave it to you?

ANNETTE. Oh, yes, dear father.

MATH. (*Rising and kissing her*) My only hope is to see you happy with Christian.

Stop MUSIC 3.

(*Enter Sozel with supper tray.*[14] *Places tray on table L.*)

(*Brightly*) And now for the supper, and some wine. (*Down R. to* WALTER *and* HANS *who have risen as if to get their coats on.*) Why don't you both stay and have a glass of wine with me?

WALTER & HANS. (*With exaggerated cordiality*) With pleasure, Burgomaster.

HANS. For your sake, Burgomaster, we will try and make that last little effort.

MATH. That's right, that's right. (*Going to table*) There's one advantage about the cold. (*Pours out wine in three glasses, a little in his own glass*) It gives one an appetite. (*All laugh.*) Here's your health.

WALTER & HANS. Yours, Burgomaster, yours.

(*All touch glasses and drink.*)

(MATHIAS *sits R. of table and proceeds to help himself to the chicken, potatoes, salt, etc.*)

MATH. (*Looking round to women who are both seated R. on stools.* CATH. *is arranging necklace on* ANNETTE's *neck.* WALTER *is seated top of table L. and* HANS. *L. of table.*) Why where's Christian, eh? Where's Christian? Hasn't he been here this evening?

ANNETTE. Oh, yes, they came to fetch him but he will return presently.

CATH. He came here late to-day in consequence of some duty he had to perform in the Hovald in the capture of some smugglers.

MATH. Hovald! B-u-r-r-! nice weather for such business as that. Why, by the side of the river I found the snow five feet deep.

ALL. Five feet deep.

MATH. (*Cutting chicken*) Yes, five feet.

WALTER. Yes, we were talking about that. We were telling the Quarter-master we hadn't seen such severe weather as this since what is called the Polish Jew's winter.

(*During this speech* MATH. *has poured out more wine and is about to drink when he stops, alarmed at "Polish Jew's winter", looks up to see if they have observed his agitation and then pretends to pick a piece of cork with his little finger and wipes it on cloth.*)

MATH. Oh, you were talking of that, were you? (*Sleigh bells*)[16] (*When he hears bells—stops.*)[17] The Bells! The Bells!

HANS. During that winter, you remember, Burgomaster, the whole valley was covered several feet deep with snow and it was a long time before the horse of the Polish Jew could be dug out.

MATH. No doubt, no doubt. That's like a grandmother's story now, and is thought of no more. (*Breaks bread, puts it in mouth, then puts it down.*)

(HANS *and* WALTER *talk together, not looking at* MATH. *He looks at them,*[18] *then at the women, then rising—*)

Don't you—don't you hear the—hear the sound of sleigh bells on the road?[19]

ALL. Sleigh bells, no.

(MATHIAS *staggers—shakes—and sits in chair R. arm over back, head on arms.*)

CATH. What's the matter, Mathias. (*Over to him, hand on his forehead*) You're cold, you're ill.

MATH. No, no, I'm well. I'm well.

CATH. Yes, yes, indeed you are. Some warm wine will restore you. Come Annette, come, we'll warm some wine by the kitchen fire. Bring the light. Come quickly.

(*Both exit R. with candle.*)

MATH. (*Rises*) (*Walks R.*)

WALTER. (*Rising, and putting on coat with* HANS) Come along Hans, we'll go and see after the horse. At the same time it's very strange, it was never discovered who did the deed.

MATH. (*Up to table*) Ay, the rogues have escaped, more's the pity. (*Hurriedly pouring out wine*) Here's your health!

WALTER & HANS. (*Drink*) Yours, Burgomaster, yours.

WALTER. Why, Hans, it's just upon the stroke of ten.

HANS. So it is, ten o'clock, I declare.

MATH. Good night, good night.

WALTER & HANS. Good night, Burgomaster, good night! Come along, we must go and look at the horse, it's a long way, etc. etc. (*Off—voices dying away*)

The 'vision scene' as depicted in *The Illustrated London News*, 23 December 1871. It shows the Jew's sleigh before the snow-swept bridge at Vechem. In the distance a burning lime-kiln glows. A hooded man, axe in hand, stalks the Jew. The Jew's face, at first averted, turns slowly downstage, his gaze fixing upon Mathias.

MATH. (*Who has sat in chair R. at table L. rises—walks quickly R. fingers in ears which he removes when R. then runs up to window, tears curtains open and looks out and closes them again.*) No one on the road, no one! (*Down C.*) What is this jangling in my ears.

MUSIC 4.

Ah, the very night—the very hour. (*Clock strikes ten.*)[20] (*Down to chair R. of table.*) I feel a darkness coming over me, a giddiness siezes me. (*Staggers, hand on chair back.*) Shall I call for help? No, no, courage, Mathias, courage. The Jew is dead—dead—ha ha ha—dead! (*Drops into chair, head in arms on table—vision slowly revealed.*[21] *Mathias rises.*) It's nothing, the wind and the cold have overcome me. (*Walks down R.*) It's nothing, nothing, nothing.

(*At the third 'nothing' Mathias has walked up C. and is confronted with full view of vision.*)

Ah, ah!

(*Loud cry dying away and falling C. as curtain descends.*) Stop MUSIC 4.

END OF ACT I[22]

The 'vision scene' as depicted by Alfred Concanen in *The Stage*, 10 December 1871. Note discrepancies in furnishings, the position of the horse, and attiude of the Jew as well as many points of agreement between the two illustrations.

THE SET FOR ACT II

The scene depicts the Burgomaster's Parlour on the morning of 26 December 1833. In contrast to the lighting of the previous act, the room is bright with sunlight which shines in through three large windows at the back. Through them we can see the village street—its houses and the church covered with snow. (This is *not* the back-cloth used for the original production at the Lyceum on 25 November 1871, which portrayed the snow-covered buildings of a comparatively large town—not a village. See Hawes Craven's sketch, page 95.)[1]

In the centre of the room, which is oak-panelled, is a large charcoal-burning stove, its flue-pipe passing through the wall. A pair of tongs and a hod of fuel are at the up-stage end of the grate; and the practicable door of the stove is hinged on the up-stage side of the opening. Right of the stove is a comfortable arm- (or elbow-) chair.

Down stage—right of centre—is a large circular table, with an elbow chair set left of it, and a smaller chair above it. Hanging over the back of the latter is Catherine's cloak.

A little above the centre of the left wall is a door—opening off stage. Below this, set against the wall, is a chair. An antique escritoire, the flap of which is closed and locked, stands against the wall down stage right, with a chair above it. Two more chairs are set against the back wall.

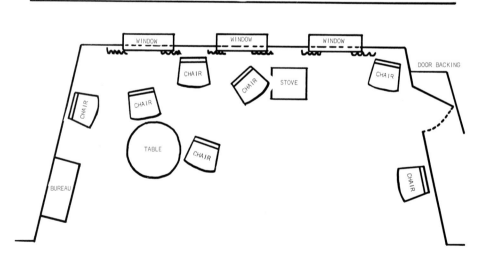

ACT II

MUSIC 5.

SCENE: Best Room in the Burgomaster's house.

MATHIAS *discovered seated L. of table C.,*[2] CATH. *at his R.,* DR ZIMMER *L.C.* CATHERINE *touches* MATHIAS's *shoulder, he looks up.*

Stop MUSIC 5.

DR. You feel better Burgomaster.

MATH. Yes, I'm well, I'm well.

DR. No more pains in the head.

MATH. No, no, no.

DR. Or strange noises in the ears.

MATH. No, no. When I tell you that I'm well—that I never was better—surely that's enough.

CATH. For a long time past, he has had bad dreams.

MATH. Hush—Hush. (*catching* CATH's *dress and pulling it*)

CATH. (*Continuing*) He talks in his sleep and his thirst has been feverish during the night.

MATH. (*Looking up at her on his R.*) Is there anything extraordinary in being thirsty during the night?

DR. Certainly not—but you *must* take more care of yourself, Burgomaster. You drink too much white wine—your attack arose entirely from this cause. You drank too much wine at your cousin's and then the blood having flown to your head—the cold seized you.

MATH. Yes, yes. I was cold it's true, but-that-stupid-gossip about the Polish Jew was the cause of it all.

DR. (*One step nearer*) How was that?

MATH. (*After looking first at* CATH. *then* DR.) Well, you must know when the Jew disappeared, they brought me the cloak and cap he had worn. I remember at the time being quite upset at the sight of them—knowing that the poor devil had been in my house. Well, since then I had never even thought of the matter until strangely enough it was brought up the night before last. It was as if I had seen the ghost of the Jew— ha-ha, one knows well enough there are no such things, and that dreams are but dreams, still one can't always—(*Suddenly to* CATH.) have you sent for the Notary?

CATH. Yes, dear, but you must keep quiet.

MATH. Quiet! I am quiet, but Annette's marriage must take place at once. When a man in robust health is liable to such attacks as these, nothing should be left until to-morrow. (*Slower*) What occurred to me the night before last might again occur to-night. I might not survive the second blow and then I should not have lived to see my dear children happy (CATH. *places L. hand on his R. shoulder—he half looks around, then petulantly*) and now leave me—whether it was the wine or the cold or the gossip about the Jew that was the cause of my attack it comes to the same thing, my mind is now at least quite clear.

DR. (*Forward a little*) But perhaps Burgomaster it would be more prudent to delay the signing of the marriage contract. You can understand the agitation....

MATH. (*Moving in chair*) Good God. Why can't people attend to their own affairs. I was ill—you bled me—good, I am well again—(*Church bell begins to ring*) so much the better. (*to Cath.*) Let the Notary be sent for at once. (CATH. *goes to chair R. of stove, picks up* DR's *hat and stick and gives them to* DR *trying to get rid of him during rest of speech.*) Let Father Walter and Hans be sent for as witnesses and let the matter be finished off without delay.

DR. (*To* CATH.) His nerves are still very much shaken. It will be better to let him have his own way. (*To* MATHIAS) Very well Burgomaster, very well; we'll say no more about it, only re-member (*at door*) be careful with the white wine.

(*Exit* DOCTOR—*door L.*)

MATH. Good! Good! (*Moving chair and under breath*) Fool!

CATH. (*Putting on cloak at door L.*) Annette! Annette!

ANNETTE. (*Off L.*) I'm coming.

MATH. Don't hurry her dear—she is dressing, you know.

CATH. But I don't take two hours to dress.

MATH. It's hardly the same thing—she expects Christian.

(*Enter* ANNETTE *door L.*)[3]

CATH. At last.

ANNETTE. Yes. I've finished at last. (*L.*)

  MUSIC 6.

I am sorry I have kept you waiting, mother.

MATH. How pretty you look.

ANNETTE. I've put on the necklace. (*Up to him*)

MATH. You have done well.

CATH. (*Getting book R.*) Come Annette, we shall be late. The service will have commenced.

ANNETTE. (*At window*) Christian hasn't come yet.

MATH. (*Chair L. of table R.*) No, possibly he's detained on duty.

CATH. (*At door*) Come Annette. (*Exit door L.*) (ANNETTE *is following slowly.*)

MATH. Annette, Annette. Have you nothing to say to me?

ANNETTE. (*Runs to him, puts arms around him*) You know, dear father how much I love you.

MATH. Yes.

CATH. (*Outside door L.*) An——nette!

MATH. Don't keep your mother waiting. She is a little impatient you know.

  (ANNETTE *kisses him, runs to door, throws kiss at him which he returns and she exits door L.*)

  MATHIAS, *left alone—sighs—rises, walks to door L., to stove, then moves up to window, sees* ANNETTE *and* CATH. *crossing L. to R. Kisses hand to them and walks down C.* SOZEL *opens window and calls.*[4]

WOMAN. (*Outside window*) Good morning, Burgomaster.

MATH. (*Looking round and not seeing her*) Good morning—Good morning—Good morning. (*Turns each time in different directions, he is now C.L. of table. R.C. he takes out snuff box and taps it forcibly—Stop MUSIC 6.*)

MATH. Everything goes well.[5] But what a lesson Mathias, what a lesson. A little more and what might not have occurred. You must have been mad. Where was your head? The mere talk of the Polish Jew to bring on such an attack. Luckily the people about here are such idiots they don't suspect anything. Well all's over now. (*Taking handkerchief from table*) But it was

'A piece of old gold! A——ah!
That came from the girdle.'

The bells—the bells again!'

that Parisian who was the real cause of my attack. The rascal had really made me nervous (*Wipes neck with handkerchief*) he wanted to send me asleep as well as the others; but I at once thought to myself: Stop! Stop! Mathias take care. This— sending you to sleep may be an invention of the devil—you might relate certain incidents in your past life. (*Smiling*) You must be cleverer than that—you must be cleverer than that. You mustn't run your neck into a halter. Ha! you will die an old man yet Mathias—you'll die an old man yet—and the most respected man in the Province (*Down C. and stop*). Only this (*Tapping snuff box and emphasising words*)—this—that since you *dream* and are apt to talk in your sleep—for the future, you will sleep in another room—alone—the key safe in your pocket. Walls have ears no doubt. (*Taking a snuff out with R. hand*) Well let them hear me as much as they please (*Taken snuff, closes box with snap and feels in pocket for keys*) and now for the marriage portion—to be given to our dear son-in-law (*Looking for key in bunch*) in order that our dear son-in-law may love us. (*Goes to bureau R. unlocks it—opens it, takes out bag of money, brings it to the table.*) Thirty thousand francs. (*Sits in chair back of table R.C., unties the bag and empties money and rouleaux out.*) Thirty thousand francs— a fine dowry for the husband of Annette. (*Counts.*) 2-4-6-8-10-12-13 Ah! (*Again counts.*) 3-5-8-13-13 (*Puts money in bag*) (*Rubs hands on coins*). Thirty thousand francs—a fine dowry for the husband of Annette—(*Counting coins into hand and placing them into bag*).[6] He's a clever fellow is Christian—a clever fellow. He's not a Kelz—half deaf—half blind—(*Trying coin*) no—no—he's a clever fellow is Christian—(*Pause*) and quite capable of getting on the right track. The first time I saw him I said to myself—you shall be my son-in-law and if anything should be discovered you will be my protector. Thirty thousand francs!! (*Counting more coins into L. hand—stops—looking at a piece of gold on table*) (*Picks up one coin*) A piece of old gold. A——ah! That came from the girdle[7] (*Drops coin*)—No—no—not for them—for me. (*Picks up coin, puts it in waistcoat pocket, wipes fingers on coat—goes to bureau R., open a drawer—takes out coin—back to table— drops coin on heap.*) (*Knee on chair*) That girdle did us a good turn, without it we were ruined. Ah, if Catherine knew—poor Catherine (*Bells*).

MUSIC 7.

The Bells—the bells again. They must come from the mill (*Rushes over to L. to door and bangs it open, calling and back to* C.). Sozel! Sozel, I say.

(*Enter* SOZEL, *book in hand* L.)

SOZEL. Did you call Burgomaster?

MATH. Is there anyone at the mill? (*Bells stop.*)

SOZEL. No, Burgomaster. (*Hides book behind her.*)

MATH. (*Taking hold of her*) No-one—are you sure?

SOZEL. Quite sure, Burgomaster.

MATH. Did not you hear the sound of bells?

SOZEL. Bells!

MATH. Yes bells, bells.

SOZEL. No, Burgomaster, I heard nothing.

Stop MUSIC 7.

MATH. (*Walking R. to C. trying to squeeze sound out of ears*) Strange, strange. (*Wiping perspiration*) (*To* SOZEL) What were you doing?

SOZEL. I was reading, Burgomaster.

MATH. What, what—ghost stories, no doubt.

SOZEL. No, Burgomaster, I was reading such a strange story— about a band of robbers being discovered after twenty-three years had passed, and all through the blade of an old knife having been found in a blacksmith's shop, hid under some old iron[8]—they captured the whole band consisting of the mother, two sons and the grandfather. They tried them and then hanged them, all in a row. Look Burgomaster, there's the picture.

(*During speech she has gradually approached* MATHIAS *and holds book right in front of him.*)

MATH. Enough, enough! (*Knocks book out of* SOZEL's *hand, who slowly picks it up.*) It's a pity you can't find something better to read. There—go—go—go!! (*Going L.*)

(SOZEL *makes a rush off. Door L.*)

MATH. Not like that[9]—not like that—(*Wiping his neck*) Am I to be caught.

(CHRISTIAN *taps at window C.*[10])

Christian! (*Goes to table and is replacing rest of rouleaux and coins in bag.*)

(*Enter* CHRISTIAN *door L. Comes C.*)

CHRIS. Ah, Burgomaster, I hope you're better.

MATH. (*Putting bag in escritoire*) Ah, Christian. I'm well. I'm well. (*Comes C. and shakes hands with him front of the table.*) Christian, I've just been counting Annette's dowry—in good sounding gold.

> (*Movement from* CHRISTIAN *who is removing gloves.*)

Ah, it was a pleasure to me to do so, for it recalled to one's memory the honest labour of days gone by.

CHRIS. I agree with you, Burgomaster, that money gained by honest industry is the only profitable wealth. It is the good seed which is sure to bring a rich harvest.

MATH. Yes, yes, I know, I know. I wish the marriage contract to be signed today.

CHRIS. Today?

MATH. Yes, the sooner the better. You know I cannot bear postponements. I can't endure people who lack decision. Once decided, why adjourn the settlement from day to day. It shows a great want of character.

CHRIS. Well, Burgomaster, nothing could be more agreeable to me than to sign at once, *but*—(MATH.—*arms on* CHRISTIAN'S *shoulders*—Well, well.) Annette.

MATH. Annette loves you and the marriage portion is ready, ah, my boy, I hope you'll be satisfied.

CHRIS. Well, you know Burgomaster, I don't bring much.

MATH. (*Hand on* CHRIS's *shoulder*) You bring courage and good conduct. (*Playfully slapping his face*) I'll take care of the rest. And now let's talk of other things. (CHRIS., *up stage, takes off sword belt, puts it with cap and gloves on chair up L.* MATH. *goes to chair R. of stove, takes paper from table and walks down, reading, to armchair R. of stove.*)[11] You were late today. Annette waited for you some time, but finding you did not come—

CHRIS. (*Interrupting*) Ah, yes, it was very strange circumstance that detained me. (*Bumps chair from L. places it in front of stove and sits*—MATHIAS *has sat in armchair R. of stove and has opened stove to feed it with coke.*) Would you believe it, Burgomaster, I've been reading over old depositions from five o'clock till ten—time passed, but the more I read the more I wanted to read.

MATH. (*Lays handkerchief on his knee*) Old depositions—to what did they refer?

CHRIS. (*Leaning forward, arms on knees, hands clasped, not looking at* MATHIAS) Why to that case of the Polish Jew (MATHIAS *is leaning down picking up coke with tongs,*[12] *drops coke and looks up. His face is illuminated with the red light from the fire*) who was murdered on the bridge of Vechem. Father Walter and Hans told me the story the day before yesterday, and I've never been able to get it out of my head. (MATHIAS *drops tongs.*) It is to me perfectly astounding that nothing was ever discovered.

MATH. (*Looking at* CHRIS. *with alarm*) No doubt, no doubt.

CHRIS. At the same time the man who committed that murder was a devilish clever fellow, for after all the efforts of the Gendarmerie, the Tribunal, and the police, not the slightest real clue was ever discovered. I read that and I am still lost in astonishment.

MATH. (*Quietly*) Yes, yes, he wasn't a fool was he? (*Takes out snuff box.*)

CHRIS. A fool. He would have made one of the cleverest Gendarmes of the Department.

MATH. (*Pinch of snuff ready*) Do you think, do you really think so?

CHRIS. Think so, I'm certain of it, (MATH. *takes snuff*) for there are so many methods of seeking out criminals in small affairs and so few escape that to commit a crime like this undetected, showed that the man possessed extraordinary address.

(MATHIAS *shuts stove.*)

MATH. You're right, Christian. You're quite right and what you say shows your good sense. Here. Here.

(CHRISTIAN *draws chair up to allow* MATH. *to touch his knees.*)

When a man has committed a crime and by it gains money, he becomes like a gambler and tries his second and his third throw. He is the cleverest rogue who, having committed one successful crime, can resist the temptation to commit another. (*Sitting back*)

CHRIS. I quite agree with you, Burgomaster, I quite agree with you. But the most extraordinary part of this affair is to me that no trace was ever discovered of the murdered man. Now do you know the idea that I have of the matter.

MATH. (*Rises, goes to table, reads paper as he talks to hide emotion.*) No—no—what—what is—what is your idea, Christian? (*Stands with back to* CHRIS.)

57

CHRIS. (*Rising and going to* MATHIAS) Well! About that time it appears there were several lime kilns burning in the neighbourhood of Vechem. (*Emphasising points by fingers on hand.*) Now I imagine that the body of the Jew after he was murdered was burnt in one of those kilns and from this cause nothing was ever found of him but the cloak and cap—now old Kelz, my predecessor, clearly never thought of that. (*Turns suddenly and looks at* MATH. *for first time during the speech.*)

MATH. (*Looking at* CHRIS.) Very likely. Very likely. (*Licking his lips as if dry with fear*) Do you know that idea certainly never entered my head, you—you—you are the first who ever suggested it.

CHRIS. (*With enthusiasm*) Yes, but this idea leads to many others. Supposing enquiry had been made as to the different people who were burning lime at that time.

MATH. (*Springing at* CHRISTIAN,[14] *seizing him by the throat with a cry of rage and forcing him into the chair he* (CHRIS.) *has been sitting in, then turning it off into a laugh of hysteria[15]—slapping him on shoulders, face and arms*) Take care, take care, why I—I—ha, ha, I myself, I had a limekiln burning at the time the crime was committed.

CHRIS. You—you Burgomaster, ha ha.

(*Both go up C. laughing in crescendo.*)

(*At beginning of* MATH.'s *laugh* VILLAGERS *pass from church R. to L. and are ready at door L. for entrance, after a slight pause* CATH. *and* ANNETTE *enter*)

MATH. (*Still laughing*) (*Coming C. and sitting in chair L. of table R. to Cath.*) Have you sent for the notary?

CATH. Yes, dear, he is here already and is reading the contract. (*Pins a wedding favour on* MATHIAS's *coat, who pats her hand.* CHRISTIAN *has gone L. to* ANNETTE)

CHRIS. (*L.C.*) How that pretty necklace becomes you, Annette.

ANNETTE. It was dear father who brought it me from Ribeauville.

CHRIS. (*Taking her hands*) It is to be today, Annette.

ANNETTE. Yes, Christian, it is to be today.

(*They converse.*)

(MATHIAS *sees them, places his fingers on his lips to* CATH. *walks quickly at back of them and says suddenly*)[16]

MATH. Well. (*They separate.*) Well you know what is customary when father, mother and everybody consents—you kiss your betrothed.

CHRIS. Is that true, Annette?

ANNETTE. I—I don't know, Christian.

(*They embrace and go up.*)

MATH. (*Crosses C. to* CATH. *seated at table R.*) Look at our children, Catherine. How happy they are. When I think we were once as happy as they are. It's true, it's true, I was as happy once! (*Sees* CATH. *crying.*) Why are you crying. You're not sorry to see this?

CATH. (*Rising and drying tears*) No—no, these are tears of joy, I can't help it.

(*He embraces her.*)

MATH. Well then, my children, everything is ready. It only remains to sign the contract. (*Crosses to door L.*) Walter, Hans, come in. Let everybody come in. The most important acts in life should always take place in the presence of others. It is an old but honest custom of Alsace.

MUSIC 8.

(*Taking snuff. Places snuff box on table.*)[17]

(*Music—enter first* SOZEL *with candelabra, lights up,* MEN, NOTARY, CLERK, 4 GIRLS *with flowers.* MATHIAS *greets them.* WALTER, HANS *and* VILLAGERS. NOTARY *goes to table R. takes contract from bag carried by clerk.* WALTER *and* HANS *shake hands with* CATH. *and* MATH. *who goes with* NOTARY *to table and reads contract*)[18]

(*Business at table of reading contract.*) Stop MUSIC 8.

NOTARY. (*At end of music*) You have all heard the reading of the marriage contract between Christian Beme, Quartermaster of Gendarmes, and Annette Mathias. Has any one any observations to make?

(*Exclamation from* VILLAGERS.)

Then we can at once take the signatures.

MATH. (*who has gone to escritoire R. and taken out bag of money and placed it on table R.*) Here is the marriage portion. It is not in promises made on paper, but in good French gold— thirty thousand francs in good French gold.

ALL—CHRIS. Thirty—thousand—francs.

CHRIS. Oh, it's too much Burgomaster.

MATH. (*Going C. to* CHRIS.) Nonsense, nonsense, Christian. And when Catherine and myself are gone there will be more—more.

(*Movement in* VILLAGERS).

And now Christian, I want you to make *one* promise.

CHRIS. (*Down L.C.* ANNETTE *on his L.* CATH. *behind* MATH. *C.*) What promise, Burgomaster?

MATH. Young men are ambitious. It is natural that they should hope to advance themselves in life. But Christian, I ask you to promise me that you will stay—remain in this village as long as we live.

(*Movement from* CHRISTIAN—*surprise.*)

You understand, we have only one child, we love her dearly and to lose her altogether would break our hearts.

(CATH. *places her hand on* MATH'*s shoulder, who looks at her and then back at* CHRIS.)

You promise?

CHRIS. (*Looks first at* ANNETTE, *who gives assent and then back at* MATH.) I promise.

MATH. Your word of honour given before all.

'And now to sign the contract.'

CHRIS. My word of honour given before all. (*Clasps* MATH. *hand with his R.*)

ALL. Ah.

MATH. (*Aside—walking R. and taking pinch of snuff*) T'was necessary. (*Aloud and walking to chair L. of table R.C.*) And now to sign the contract.

(NOTARY *hands him a pen which* MATH. *takes—*NOTARY *shows him where to sign.* MATH. *puts pen to paper when* BELLS *are heard—he looks around L. back to R. when he notices notary looking at him with astonishment. He asks him the meaning of a sentence in contract. The* NOTARY *introduces his clerk who tells him.* MATH. *shakes hands with him and signs, raising his R. hand with pen in it to head. Bells stop, he rises, calls* CHRISTIAN, *who does not here him, calls him again.*)

Christian, sign—sign, my boy. (*Hands him the pen and* WALTER *comes C. through group and calls out.*)

WALTER. It's not every day you sign a contract like that.

(*Digs him in the ribs*[20]—VILLAGERS *laugh.*)

(CHRISTIAN *signs, turns and gives pen to* CATH. *who makes her cross.*) (MATHIAS *pours a drink from water bottle, drinks it.* CHRIS. *refuses drink.*)

60

MATH. (*Tapping table with snuff-box*) Annette, Annette.

(ANNETTE *signs, is congratulated by* VILLAGERS.)

MATH. (*Going R. aside*) Now if the Jew should return, Christian must drive him back again. (*Aloud*) And now one waltz—one waltz, and then to dinner.

ALL. Ay—ay.

WALTER. (*Coming through* C.) Stop! Stop! Let's first have the song of the betrothed.

MUSIC 9.

ALL. Ay—ay.

ANNETTE. *Air (Lauterbach)*[21]
Suitors of wealth and high degree,
In style superbly grand
Tended their love on bended knee
And sought to win my hand.

(*Tyrolienne* [22] *by all and waltz*)

But a soldier brave came to woo.
No maid such love could spurn—
Proving his heart was fond and true
Won my love in return.

(*Tyrolienne, as before, by all and waltz*)

(*They choose partners and arrange themselves during introduction. When music begins*[23] MATHIAS *dancing a step goes to chair L. of table and sits.*) (*Then song and dance.*) (*Two verses are sung. At the end of the second chorus Bells are heard,* MATH. *who has been seated C. starts up.*)

MATH. The Bells! The Bells!

(*Throws his arms in the air.* CATH. *sees him, runs toward him. He seizes her, waltzes madly round and round with her as he shouts*)

Ring on! Ring on! (*The last 'on' being a prolonged hysterical shriek*)

QUICK CURTAIN   Stop MUSIC 9.

END OF ACT II

61

THE SETS FOR ACT III

ACT III, SCENE I. THE BURGOMASTER'S BEDROOM

The walls are panelled from floor to ceiling in dark oak. The back wall being painted on a gauze cloth. There is a door left opening off stage. In the right wall is a curtained alcove behind which is seen a bed. A small circular table down right by alcove, with a chair left of it. On the table, a carafe of water and a glass. Two chairs are set against the back wall. (See ground plan.)

ACT III, SCENE 2. A COURT OF JUSTICE

The walls of the Court are of dark grey stone with a high vaulted ceiling. Right is a large archway (see ground plan).

The Judge's bench is of dark oak. So is the Court furniture. The scene is dimly lighted as in a dream and played behind a gauze (the back wall of the previous bedroom scene).

Note: See instructions on silence and lighting in text. They are very important.

ACT III, SCENE 3. THE BURGOMASTER'S BEDROOM

It being about ten o'clock in the morning, the sun is shining. As the windows are in the 'fourth wall' the main source of light will come from the floats.

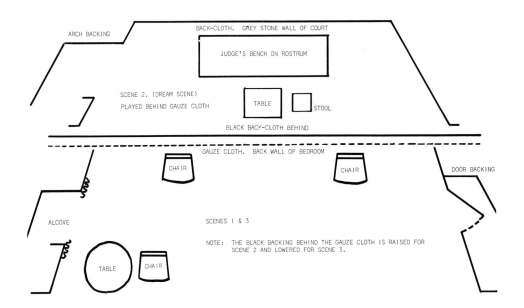

ACT III

SCENE: Room in Burgomaster's House.

(MUSIC 10. To take up curtain off R. Song to take up twice ff. once pp.)

Doorway or alcove O.P. behind which is seen a bed, and covered with curtains, small table down R. by alcove on which is a bottle of water and glass. One chair R.

TIME: Night.

(MUSIC 10 Chorus three times)

(Enter L.D. after second chorus SOZEL *with a lighted candle,[1] which she places on small table R. There must be an extinguisher attached to it. Enter* MATHIAS *and* CATHERINE, FATHER WALTER *and* HANS, *arm in arm, a little intoxicated.* CATHERINE *places chair for* MATHIAS. *Business.)[2]*

HANS. (*Laughing*) Ha, Ha! Everything has gone off admirably. We only wanted something to wind up well with, and I may say that we are all as well wound up as the great clock of Strasbourg.

(Violin Solo 10)[3]

WALTER. What wine we have drunk! For many a day we shall remember the signing of Annette's marriage contract! Ha, ha, ha! I should like to witness such a contract every second day.

HANS. There I object to your argument. Every day I say!

(Enter CHRISTIAN *and* ANNETTE)

CHRIS. (*Crosses to* MATHIAS.) And so you are determined, Mathias, to sleep here to-night?

MATH. Yes, I am decided. I know what is best for me. The heat was the cause of my accident—this room is cooler, and will prevent its recurrence.

(Distant laughter off L. by KARL, TONY *and* FRITZ.)

HANS. Listen how they are still revelling! Come, Father Walter, let us rejoin them downstairs. Come along, come along! Let's rejoin them!

(*Violin Solo 9 off R.*)[4]

WALTER. But Mathias already deserts us—just at the moment when we were beginning to thoroughly enjoy ourselves.

MATH. (*Seated R.C.*) What more do you wish me to do? From noon to midnight is surely enough.

WALTER. (*C.*) Enough it may be, but not too much. Never too much of such wine, say I!

HANS. (*L.C.*) There again I object to your argument—never enough I say!

CATH. (*L.C.*) Oh, no, no, no! Mathias is right—you remember Doctor Zimmer told him to be careful of the wine he took, or it would one day play him false, and he has already had too much since the morning.

MATH. One glass of water before I go to bed is all that I require. It will calm me, it will calm me.

(*Laughter again L. and*

Enter at door L. KARL, FRITZ *and* TONY.[5] *They are slightly merry and push up against one another, filling up the doorway.*)

(*End of solo—applause etc.*)

KARL, FRITZ & TONY. Good night, Burgomaster! Good night!

TONY. I say, Hans! Don't you know that the night watchman is below?

HANS. The night watchman! What in the name of all that is political does he want?

KARL. He requires us all to leave and the house to be closed. It is past hours, you know.

MATH. Give him his fill of wine, give him all he wants—and then good night all!

WALTER. Past hours! For a Burgomaster, no regulations ought to exist.

HANS & OTHERS. No, no, no! Certainly not!

MATH. (*Firmly and authoritatively*) Regulations made for all must be obeyed by all.

WALTER. (*In an undertone, subdued*) Well, we'd better go.

(MATHIAS *gives directions to* CATH. *to send them away.*)

CATH. (*To* WALTER) Don't thwart his wish! Say good night to
him and go home. Follow his directions.

WALTER. (*Shaking hands with* MATHIAS) Good night, Mathias!
I wish you calm repose—and no bad dreams!

MATH. (*Fiercely*) I never dream![6] (*Mildly*) Good night all!

(*Betrothal Chorus—MUSIC 9—twice.*)

(*Exeunt* KARL, FRITZ *and* TONY *D.L.*)

KARL, FRITZ & TONY. (*As they exeunt*) Good night, Burgomaster—
good night.

MATH. (*When they are off*) Good night, Walter! Good night,
Hans!

(*Exeunt* WALTER, HANS *and* SOZEL *with candle.*)

MUSIC 11.

(*Blue Foots down and out.*)

(*To* CATH.) Good night. (*Embracing her*) I shall be better here,
the wine, the riot, these songs have quite dazed my brain! I
shall *sleep* better here! I shall *sleep* better!

'... the wine, the riot, these songs have quite dazed my brain.'

(CATH. *goes L. to door*)

CHRIS. Yes, this room is fresh and cool. Good night; good night, Annette!

MATH. Good night, Christian—good night the same to you!

(*They shake hands*, CHRIS. *crosses to L. kisses* CATH. *and exit L.*)

ANNETTE. (*Going to* MATHIAS) Good night, dear father! (*Kisses him.*) May you sleep well!

MATH. (*Kissing her affectionately*) My child! (*Business with* ANNETTE.)

(*Exeunt* CATH. *and* ANNETTE *L.D.*) *Stop MUSIC 11.*

(*When they are gone*, MATHIAS *rises, listens, goes to door L. locks it.*)[7]

At last I am alone! (*Locking door*) To-night I shall sleep without a fear haunting me! If any new danger should threaten the father-in-law of the Quartermaster it would soon be averted. Ah! what a power it is to know how to guide your destiny in life! You must hold good cards in your hand, good cards, as I have done. If you play them well, you may defy ill fortune.

(*MUSIC 10—repeat—Chorus ff. Chord quietly by violin in A Major off L.3.E.*)

CHORUS
(*This is sung by two parts, taken up at regular intervals*)
Now since we must part, let us drain a last glass,
    Let us drink!
Let us first drink to this gentle young lass,
    Let us drink!
From others this toast, we'll none of us shrink,
Others shall follow when we've time to think,
Our burden shall be, let us drink,
The burden to bear is good drink!

(*Loud laughter*)

MATH. (*Pours water in glass.*) Ha! ha! Those jolly topers have all they want! What holes they will make in the snow before they reach their homes! (*Drinking and replacing glass on pedestal*) Drink! Drink! Strange? To drink and drive away remorse! Yes, everything goes well! (*Puts watch down. During this speech takes off coat and vest and appearing slightly under the influence of wine.*) Mathias, you can at least boast of having well managed your affairs! The contract signed—rich—prosperous—respected—happy! (*Business with waistcoat.*) No

66

one will hear you if you dream—no one! No more folly, no more dreams, no more Bells! (*Throws waistcoat on chair.*) Tonight I triumph! for conscience is at rest!

(MUSIC *10 and Chorus repeated three times, then three chords pp. and dies away*
during which MATHIAS *having divested himself of his coat and vest,[8] goes into alcove R. closing the curtains—After Chorus dies away, the MUSIC 12 in Orchestra commences.*)

(*As* MATHIAS *puts candle out, Blue lens L. shelf out with shutter quickly, then turn out at switch.*)

(*After a pause,* MATHIAS's *arm is seen[9] to extend out from the curtains and puts the extinguisher on the candle.*)

(*When* MATHIAS *is in situation, take up cloth behind painted gauze and discover the*

COURT VISION[10]

(PRESIDENT *in robes C. at back.* JUDGES *R. and L. of him.* CLERK OF COURT *in L. corner below him.* THREE COUNSEL OF BARRISTERS *in seats R. and L.* SPECTATORS (MALE & FEMALE) *R. above them.[11]* GENDARMES *R.U.E. and L. corner. Large table C. on which is the Jew's cloak and hat.*) (*Stop MUSIC 12.*)

Backing

	JUDGE	PRESIDENT	JUDGE	
	○	○	○	
GENDARME				GENDARME
○				○
BARRISTER				desk
○				
BARRISTER				
○		table		
BARRISTER		MATHIAS		
○		on stool		
		○		

Painted Gauze[12]

chair   chair

door

bed

alcove

table

L.

67

(Perfect silence must be observed during this scene to give effect to the performance.[13]

(Sledge Bells ready L.)

(The Court is lighted by Lime Lights from O.P. flies, and the lights must follow MATHIAS *during his action throughout the scene.)*[14]

(As the Scene is discovered, MATHIAS *dressed as in Vision of Act I is seated dejected on stool L. of table.* THE CLERK *standing up L. holding a roll of paper in his hand, as if after reading the indictment.)*

(As CLERK *speaks:—*
   1 Dia on MATHIAS *from R. flies.*
* *1 Dia L. flies for crowd.   or stage*
* *1 Dia L. flies for Judges.   ditto*
(These lights come on and off [as cued].

CLERK. Therefore, the prisoner Mathias is accused of 'having, on the night of the 24th of December, 1818, between midnight and one o'clock, assassinated the Jew Koveski, upon the Bridge of Vechem, to rob him of his gold'.

PRESIDENT. Prisoner, you have heard the act of accusation read.

   (Lights on.)

You have already heard the depositions of the witnesses— What have you to say in answer?

MATH. *(Violently and rising)* Do you call such people witnesses? People who heard nothing. People who live miles from the place where the crime was committed. At night, and in the winter time! You call such people witnesses!

PRES. Answer with calmness—this violence will avail you nothing. You are a man full of cunning.

MATH. *(With humility)* No—no—no—I am a man of simplicity.

PRES. You knew well the time to select; you knew well how to evade all suspicion; you knew well how to destroy all direct evidence; you are a dangerous man!

MATH. *(Derisively)* Because nothing can be proved against me I am dangerous! Therefore, every honest man then is dangerous when nothing can be proved against him! A rare encouragement for honesty!

PRES. The Public Voice accuses you! Answer me this—how is it that you hear the sound of Bells?

MATH. *(Passionately)* I do not hear the sound of bells!

(*Bells pp. L.U.E.*)

(MATHIAS *starts and trembles.*)

PRES. You answer falsely! At this moment you hear that sound. Tell us why is this?

MATH. It is nothing! Nothing! 'Tis but a jangling in my ears.

PRES. Unless you acknowledge the true cause of this sound you hear, to explain the matter to us we shall summon the Mesmerist.

MATH. (*Suddenly and defiantly*) It's true, it is true then—that I hear this sound—

(*Lights off—Bells stop.*)

PRES. (*To* CLERK) Write that down.

MATH. Yes; but I hear it in a dream.

PRES. Write that he hears it in a dream!

MATH. (*Furiously*) Is it a crime to dream? (*Turns appealingly to* SPECTATORS *R. and L.*) Listen, friends! Do not fear for me! All this is but a dream! If it were not a dream, should I be clothed in this dress? Should I have before me such Judges as these—Judges, who acting upon their own empty ideas, would hang a fellow creature—Ha, ha, ha! It is a dream! A dream! Ha, ha.

PRES. Silence, Prisoner! (*Addressing his Fellow* JUDGES.) Gentlemen, the Jew's horse carried bells, and this sound arises in the prisoner's mind from a remembrance—

MATH. It's false!

PRES. . . . . the remembrance of what is past—the memory of what he would conceal from us.

MATH. It is false! I have no memories!

PRES. Be silent!

(*Lights on.*)

MATH. (*Enraged*) I'll not be silent! A man cannot be condemned on such suppositions—you must have proofs!

(*At this point* MATHIAS *is standing with his hand on the Jew's cloak and cap on table.*)

(*1 Dia. quickly on cloak—Gently remove it on to* MATHIAS *and follow with other all through scene.*)

PRES. You are looking upon the cloak and cap of the murdered man. What have you to say?

MATH. I do not—I do not hear the sound of bells!

PRES. You see, gentlemen, the prisoner contradicts himself; he has already made the avowal—now he retracts it.

MATH. No—no—no; I hear nothing! I hear *nothing*!

> (*Bells pp. L.*)

> (*Distractedly, his hands covering his ears*) It is the blood rushing to my brain, this jangling in my ears! (*Fiercely*) I ask for Christian! Why is not Christian here? He'll prove that I'm an honest man!

PRES. Do you persist in your denial?

MATH. (*Fiercely*) I do! I do! Nothing can be proved against me! It is a gross injustice to keep an honest man in prison—I suffer in the cause of Justice!

> (*Bells cease.*)

PRES. You persist?

MATH. (*Solemnly, hearing the Bells have ceased*) I do! I do!

PRES. Well considering that since this murder took place fifteen years have passed, and that it would be impossible to throw light upon the circumstances by ordinary means—First, through the cunning and audacity of the prisoner, and Secondly, through the death of witnesses who might have given evidence—we therefore decree that the Court hear the Mesmerist.

MATH. I oppose it!

PRES. Summon the Mesmerist![15]

MATH. I oppose it!

PRES. Summon the Mesmerist!

MATH. (*In a terrible voice*) Dreams prove nothing.

PRES. Summon the Mesmerist!

MATH. It is in defiance of all Justice!

PRES. (*Calmly*) If you are innocent, why should you fear the Mesmerist? Because he can read the inmost secrets of your heart!

> (MATHIAS *despairingly droops his head on his hands leaning against barrier at back by* GENDARMES.)

Be calm, or believe me your own indiscretion will prove that you are guilty!

> (*Lights off altogether. Pause.*)

MATH. (*Suddenly, as with an idea*) I demand an Advocate! I wish to instruct the advocate Linder of Saverne—in a case like this

I do not care for cost—I am calm, as calm as any man who has no reproach against himself—I fear nothing! But dreams are dreams! (*Loudly*) I ask for Christian! Why is Christian not here? My honour is his honour! Let him be sent for; he will prove that I am an honest man! Christian! Christian! I have made you rich, come, come and defend me!

(*MUSIC 13.*)

(*Enter* MESMERIST *R.U.R.*[16] *who comes down R.* MATHIAS *glaring at him from L. of table.*)

'Who can believe in the follies of the Mesmerist, they only deceive people.'

MESMERIST. (*Bowing to the Court*) (*Stop MUSIC 13.*) President and Judges of the Court! it is your decree that has brought me before your tribunal. Without such direction terror alone would have kept me far from here.

MATH. (*Derisively*) Who can believe in the follies of the Mesmerist, they only deceive people for the purpose of gaining money—they merely perform the tricks of conjurors. I have seen this fellow already at my cousin's at the Fair at Ribeauville.

PRES. (*To* MESMERIST) Can you send this man to sleep?[17]

(MATHIAS *looks into the face of the* MESMERIST. *The* MESMERIST *looks at* MATHIAS *steadfastly, at last* MATHIAS *is unable to bear his fixed look and droops his head upon his breast before the* MESMERIST *and sits on stool L. of table.*)

MES. I can!

MATH. (*Rising*) You cannot. I will not be made the subject of this imposter's experiment.

PRES. I command it.

MATH. Christian! Where is Christian? Why is not Christian here? He will prove that I am an honest man.

PRES. Your resistance betrays you!

MATH. (*In a subdued but determined tone and manner*) I have no fear—I have no fear! (*MUSIC 14*) (*Sits resolutely on stool L.*) Courage, Mathias, courage! If you sleep you are lost! Courage, courage—

'Mathias, courage! If you sleep you are lost!' Sir Henry Irving in the 'dream scene', by Charles Buchel in *The Tatler*, 30 July 1902.

(*The* MESMERIST *goes up R. looking at* MATHIAS *and comes down behind him L. and makes passes—gradually* MATHIAS *succumbs under the influence.*)

No, no—I will not sleep![18] I will—(*Faintly*) I—will—not—no—(*Becomes fixed, his eyes open and staring on vacancy.*)

(*Stop MUSIC 14.*)

MES. He sleeps! What shall I ask him? (*Goes up L.*)

PRES. Ask him what he did on the night of the 24th of December fifteen years ago?

MES. (*In a firm voice to* MATHIAS) You are at the night of the 24th of December, 1818—

MATH. (*In a low voice*) Yes.

MES. What time is it?

MATH. Half-past eleven!

MES. Speak on—I command you.

(MATHIAS *continues, as if describing a Vision presented to his eyes.*)

MATH. The people are leaving the Inn—Catherine and little Annette have gone to rest—our man Kaspar comes in, he tells me that the Lime Kiln is lighted—I answer him 'It is well—go to bed. I will see to the Kiln.' He leaves me! I am alone with the Jew, who warms himself at the stove—outside, everything sleeps—nothing is heard except from time to time the Jew's horse under the shed when he shakes his bells.

(*Pause.*)

MES. Of what are you thinking?

MATH. I am thinking that I must have money—that if I have not 2000 francs by the 31st, the Inn I hold will be taken from me— I am thinking that no one is stirring, that it is night, that there are two feet of snow upon the ground, and that the Jew must follow the high road—quite—alone!

MES. Have you already decided to attack him?

MATH. (*After a short silence*) That man is strong—he has broad shoulders. No! I am thinking he would defend himself well should anyone attack him.

MES. What ails you?

'He looks at me—he has grey eyes.... I'll do it.'

MATH. He looks at me—he has grey eyes.[19]

MES. You are decided?

MATH. Yes, yes, I'll do it. I will risk it!

MES. Go on!

MATH. I must look around though. I go out—all is silent: all is dark: The snow still falls. No one will trace my footsteps. (*Raises his hands as if feeling for something.*)

MES. What are you doing?

MATH. I am feeling in the sleigh should he carry pistols! There is nothing! I will do it! (*Listens*) All is silent *in the village*! Our little Annette is crying. A goat bleats in the stable—the Jew is walking in his room.

MES. You re-enter?

MATH. Yes; he's placed six francs upon the table. I return him his change—he fixes his eyes steadily upon me.

MES. He speaks to you?

MATH. He asks me how far it is to Mutzig. Four leagues! I wish him well on his journey. He answers, 'God bless you.' (*His countenance now undergoes a change.*) The girdle! He goes out! He is gone! The axe! Where is the axe? Ah! here behind the door. (*Bends down getting it.*) How cold it is! The snow falls! Not a star! Courage, Mathias, you shall possess the girdle! Courage! Courage! Courage!

MES. You follow him?

MATH. Yes, yes—I have crossed the fields—here's the Bridge, and there below the frozen rivulet—how the dogs howl at Daniel's Farm![20] How they howl! And old Frantz's forge—how brightly it glows upon the hillock. Kill a man! Kill a man! You will not do that, Mathias—you will not do that! Heaven forbids it! (*Walking L.*) Ah, you are a fool! Listen, you will be rich, your wife and child will no longer want for anything—you will pay all you owe—you will be in debt no more—it must be that I kill him! (*Back to table. Pause.*) No one on the road! No one on the road! No one! What dreadful silence! (*Wipes his forehead with his hand.*) You are hot, Mathias, you're hot, you have run too fast across the fields! How your heart beats! How it beats! The moon shines out. The clock strikes! One! One! One! The Jew has passed! He's passed, thank God! Thank God! Thank God! (*Sinks by table on his knees, head in hands.*)

(*Bells pp. L.*)

(*A pause, he listens, starts up.*) The Bells! The Bells! He comes! He comes! (*He bends down as if listening, in a low voice.*) You will be rich! You will be rich! You will be rich![21] (*Backs up R., then suddenly as if following something, springs forward and gives two terrific blows, accompanied by a savage yell.*)

(*Bells stop.*)

(MATHIAS *leans forward, and gazes on the ground in terror, extends his hands as if to touch something, draws back quickly.*)

'The Bells! The Bells! He comes! He comes! You will be rich ... you will be rich.'

73

'The horse has fled with the sleigh.' By Bernard Partridge, 1898.

Ah!!! He is dead!!!

(*Bells.*)

(*Raises himself with a deep sigh of relief, and looks round.*) The horse has fled with the sleigh! (*Listens.*) The horse has fled with the sleigh! (*Kneeling over the body.*) Quick! Quick! The girdle! The girdle! Ha, ha! (*He in action takes the girdle from the body and buckles it round his own waist.*) It is full! Full of gold! Quite full! (*Pause.*) Quick! Quick! Carry him away! (*Three times he bends down and appears to lift the body, and walks a step or two appearing as though bearing a weight.*)

MES. Where are you going?

MATH. (*Stopping*) To the Lime Kiln. I am there! (*He throws the body on the ground, and staggers back to table.*) How heavy he was! (*Sees blood on hands—breathing hard. He then bends down and pretends to lift up the Jew and throw him into the fire.*) Go into the fire, Jew! Go into the fire! (*He appears to push the body by the aid of an imaginary pole, falls over R.*) You are a fool! You are a fool! (*He crawls on hands and knees towards the Kiln and looks in, then with a terrific shriek falls back.*) Look! Look! Look! Look! Look! Look! Ah! Those eyes! Those eyes! How they glare at me! (*He appears unable to resist looking into the Kiln. He gradually becomes quiet and rests on stool, arm over stool, head on arm.*)

PRES. It is well. (*To the* CLERK) Have you written all?

CLERK. All!

PRES. (*To* MESMERIST) Awake him now, and let him read himself.

(*The* MESMERIST *takes the influence from off* MATHIAS *who gradually awakes.*)

MATH. (*Very quietly, bewildered*) What is the matter? Where am I? (*Looks around.*) Ah! yes! What is going on? What's going on? What's going on?

CLERK. (*Advances to his side L. and hands him a paper*) Here is your deposition. Read it!

MATH. (*Takes it and after reading a few lines, trembles violently.*) Fool! Fool! You have told all! You are lost.

PRES. You have heard and seen—he has condemned himself—

MATH. (*Enraged, starting up and up to* JUDGES C.) It is false! You are a set of rogues! Christian! Where is Christian! They will not let my only witness speak! Christian! Christian! They

74

would kill the father of your wife! Help me! Help me! Christian, help me! etc. (*Hanging on table, arms outstretched, face down.*)

PRES. Prisoner, you force me to speak of an event concerning which I had wished to remain silent. Your son-in-law, Christian, upon hearing of the crime with which you are charged, by his own hand sought his death! He is no more!

(MATHIAS *appears stupefied and overcome.*)

(*After consulting the other* JUDGES, *rises, solemnly*) Considering that on the night of the 24th of December 1818, Mathias committed the crime of assassination upon the person of one Koveski, a Polish Jew, we therefore decree that the said Mathias, be hanged by the neck until he is dead!

MUSIC 15.

(*Large bell tolls the Death Knell one, big knocks 3. Seven knocks twice up stage, repeated by several knocks twice at door L.*)

(*At bell, all lights out quickly.*)

(*The dark cloth comes down.*)

When lights up SEGUE.

ORIGINAL SCENE
[Setting as at beginning of Act III]

(SEGUE)

(*Marriage Bells strike up a merry peal. Pause.*)[22]

(*As Marriage Bells ring out, Foots Blue Full*) (*2 cir.*) (*switch*)
(*1 Blue Lens L. shelf*)
(*3 white borders full*) Then

(CHRISTIAN *and* OTHERS *heard at D.L. loudly knocking— This knocking kept up for some time.*)

CHRIS. (*Outside L. between the knocks*) Mathias! Mathias! (*Pause. Knocks.*) How soundly he sleeps! Mathias! Mathias!

WALTER. (*Without*) Mathias! Mathias! (*Knocking*)

VOICES. (*In general Chorus*) Mathias! Burgomaster! Burgomaster!

CHRIS. (*Increased knocking*) Wake, Mathias! Mathias! Arise! Wake! Shall I break open the door?

ALL. Yes.

CHRIS. Give me that gun! Stand back!

(CHRIS., *with increased hammering at the door, and the noise till the door is forced off its hinges, and hurled on the stage.*)

MUSIC 16.

(CHRIS. *rushes in, goes quickly to alcove, opens curtains with his hands, looks in, starts back in horror—closes them and half turning, waves back the* OTHERS.)

(*Enter hurriedly with* CHRIS. D.L. CATH., ANNETTE, HANS, SOZEL *and* WALTER.)

CATH. (C.) What has happened? Christian, speak! What has happened? (*She rushes towards alcove.*)

CHRIS. (*Warning her back*) Do no come near! Do not come near!

(CATHERINE *endeavouring to go past him*)

HANS

○

CHRIS.

○

CATHERINE   ANNETTE

○   ○

(As CHRIS. *speaks to* CATH., *they gradually get over to C. leaving R. of stage open, as*

BELLS *as* MATHIAS *rushes in till Curtain down.*)

(MATHIAS *rushes on dressed as he was at the time he retired behind the curtains. His eyes are fixed, and his appearance deathly and haggard. He clutches the drapery convulsively, and staggers with a yell to C., is caught in the arms of* CHRIS., *who places him in chair brought forward to C. hastily by* HANS. MATHIAS *sinks in chair, holds one hand to* ANNETTE *L. then to* CHRIS. *R.*)

MATH. Take the rope from my neck—take—the—rope—neck— (*Struggles and dies.*)[23]

(CATH. *and* ANNETTE *kneel.*)

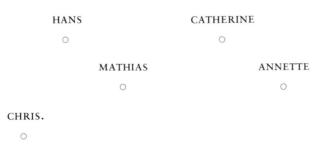

SLOW CURTAIN

'Take the rope from my neck.' This photograph as published by the London Stereoscopic Company was printed in reverse, a finding confirmed by observing Irving's hair parting (on the left side in all other photographs), by consulting Irving's stage directions, and by a drawing of the same moment by Phil May, privately owned. Here the photograph is reversed again to give the correct impression.

TIME

ACT I.	24 minutes
ACT II.	28 minutes
ACT III.	35 minutes

1 hour 27 minutes.

Waits, after Act I, 8 minutes
after Act II, 6 minutes

1 hour 41 minutes

SNOW PROPERTIES

Cotton wool on stage under Horse.

Cotton wool on cap, sleeves and coat of Jew.

Cotton wool on Mathias' Double.

Salt on hats and clothes of CHRISTIAN, HANS & FATHER WALTER

Soap on MATHIAS's and on boots of ALL in First Act.

NOTE [recipe for 'snow']

¼ lb. Common Yellow soap.
A small piece of Soda.
3 pints of water.

all boiled together, then churned in machine till thick.

NOTES

NOTE TO SCENE DESCRIPTIONS

Stage Cloths. From my position in the third row of the stalls at the Grand, Boscombe, I couldn't see these. But at the Queen's Theatre in 1909 we were in the front row centre of the Dress Circle and I recall the following. *Act I:* dark brown floor boards. No carpet. Only the mat at the Inn door. *Act II:* dark brown floor boards; large deep crimson-coloured carpet in centre of room. *Act III: Scene 1.* Dark oak floor cloth. Large brown rug covering greater part of acting area. *Scene 2.* Dark grey stone floor. Only seen when fly limes lit various areas.   (E.J.–E.)

ACT I

1. *Hans (filling pipe and laughs).* Hans smokes a 'German-shaped' pipe. This is a long-stemmed pipe dropping downward to a deep ornamented bowl of meerschaum, cherry, or briar, which he fills from a pouch in his pocket although there is on the table a lighted candle and a tray with a tobacco-jar and spills.   (D.M.)

2. *Loud gust of wind.* Although Catherine refers to a gust of wind, the wind was kept moaning throughout the act. It wasn't kept on a single level, however, but rose and fell. They knew how to work wind machines to produce sudden blow-ups then fading away again. The wind suddenly gusting with a swirl of snow flakes as the outside door opened created a memorably eerie mood. You could feel the cold.   (E.J.-E.)

3. *Wood and glass crash*, R. '. . . the playgoer's imagination plays a considerable part in the matter. For example, the first time I saw Irving's Mathias in *The Bells* was from a hot and densely crowded Lyceum pit on a summer night in the 'eighties, and the thing that frightened me most that evening happened before Irving had even appeared . . . It will be remembered that early in the first act, before the haunted burgomaster has appeared, two village cronies are sitting by the fire in the inn-parlour gossiping about the snowstorm, and the murder of twenty-five years [*sic*] before, while Madame Mathias sits knitting. Suddenly a crash is heard from outside, and the burgomaster's wife hurries off to see what has happened. Presently she returns to say that it had been

nothing worse than her stupid maid, Sozel, letting a plate fall and smashing it. [See Catherine, p. 43: 'Sozel had left the windows in the kitchen open, and now every pane of glass in them is broken.'] Afterwards, when Mathias appeared, we had, of course, far more alarming things than that to sit through; and for days I was haunted by the jingle of the sleigh-bells, the scream of the conscience-stricken man at the sight of the ghost at the end of the first act, the look on his face as he caught sight of the gold coin in Annette's dowry, the anguish of the dream, and the realism of the death-scene at the end. But I still remember with a smile that when the early crash came, I jumped at least an inch out of my seat!' (H. M. Walbrook, *A Playgoer's Wanderings* (London, 1926), pp. 50–1).

4. *Music 2.* Music cue 2 in practice actually begins somewhat ahead of Walter's 'Well, he deserves …'. The entrance is timed for the crescendo chord synchronising with the inn door being flung open. The original *warning* cue was: '… born under a lucky star.' (D.M.)

5. *Mathias passes the window.* Mathias isn't seen clearly through the window as he enters from the snowstorm. Until he enters the room in a gust of snow, he is only a dim figure. (E.J.-E.)

6. *Mathias enters.* 'Irving, once on, the shout of applause going up, he lowers his arms, he lowers his head, he relaxes his force all over, seems to turn it off to an almost dead calm, while the applause rolls on and up. Twice, maybe three times, he, as it were, shifts one foot (his right I think it was), and by this slight and meaningless gesture a limit is reckoned to the applause which goes on and on—no other motion, except that the foot in shifting sends a slight vibration also without significance, through the whole person before us—and then as the applause dies away, at the first sign of it dying, the actor clips it off by a sudden gesture of awakening from his long and patiently endured ordeal—flings cap and whip to the right and left, and begins to shed his coat, his muffler, as his wife and daughter run to help him off with them' Edward Gordon Craig, *Henry Irving* (London, 1930), pp. 56–7.

My first glimpse of Irving was to see that pale face with a half-smile as he stood in the doorway with his arms flung wide. In one hand he held a riding whip. In the London Stereoscopic Company's photograph (page 44) of Irving's entrance he wears a fur beret. By 1880, when my father first saw *The Bells*, Irving had changed this hat for the round otter-skin cap depicted in the watercolour sketch of Irving by Bransby Williams (frontis). It was that cap I saw on 4 February 1905. Austin Brereton's *Life of Henry Irving* includes a drawing showing Irving in the cap, fur coat and crimson muffler (vol. II, p. 21). According to my father, who had seen *The Bells* at least fifty times, Irving flung his whip and hat straight across to Sozel and embraced Catherine. When I saw Irving he omitted tossing the whip, and my father remarked on this omission. (E.J.-E.)

7. *Snow removal.* Henry Irving used a hand brush to remove snow from his leggings and boots. H.B. used a long-handled birch broom. Both shook and

brushed the snow from their fur coats with their hands which were gloved. (E.J.-E.)

8. *Mathias's first movements.* As Mathias removes his crimson muffler he shakes hands with Walter and Hans over the table, then gives the coat to Catherine. Annette meanwhile removes the chair from right of the table to centre stage. (E.J.-E.)

9. *Mathias ... staring out as if impressed ...* To return to the moment after the first entrance: The process of getting rid of his coat, and brushing off the snow as he stands on the mat by the door being over, he works his way down to a chair in the centre (Irving was always in the centre—he had no inferiority complex), and there, taking off his boots, he begins to put on and buckle his shoes.

'Now you might think that the act of taking off some boots could be done in one way only—but the way Irving did it had never been though of till he did it, and has never been done since.

'It was, in every gesture, every half move, in the play of his shoulders, legs, head, and arms, mesmeric in the highest degree—showly we were drawn to watch every inch of his work as we are drawn to read and linger on every syllable of a strangely fine writer.

'While he is taking off the boots and pulling on the shoes the men at the table, who are smoking and drinking lazily, are telling in drawling tones that just before he came in they were saying that they did not remember a night like this since what was called the Polish Jew's winter.' (Here E. G. Craig becomes forgetful, for the discussion is not of 'the Polish Jew's winter' but of the mesmerist who has caused people to speak of matters that 'weigh upon their conscience'. Mathias then gives Annette the gift of a necklace, an action which holds his fear at bay. It is only after this respite from fear, as Mathias prepares to eat his supper and take a final glass of wine with the departing Hans and Walter, that the conversation turns to the snow and the Polish Jew.) (D.M.)

'By the time the speaker had got this slowly out—and it was dragged purposely—Irving was buckling his second shoe, seated, leaning over it with his two long hands stretched down over the buckles. We suddenly saw these fingers stop their work; the crown of the head suddenly seemed to glitter and become frozen—and then, at the pace of the slowest and most terrified snail, the two hands, still motionless and dead, were seen to be coming up the side of the leg [*sic*] ...' (E. G. Craig, *Henry Irving*, pp. 58–9).

10. *Business with boots, shoes and shoehorn.* Only Henry Irving and H. B. Irving used the business of removing boots by drawing them off with the toe of his other foot against the heel. He slips on his left-hand shoe, then with one hand embraces Annette, who stands to his left and with the other hand Catherine, who stands to his right, talking to them of the entertainment he has seen at Ribeauville. As he recalls the mesmerist, he imitates with a waving motion of one arm only, the mesmerist's gestures. It is the right hand and arm he uses. (E.J.-E.)

11. *Henry Irving's reaction to talk of mesmerist.* In response to Hans's recollection of a mesmerist causing his subject to tell what is on their consciences, Irving listens intently, then holds a long (10–12 seconds) pause before responding in a low voice, 'Exactly.'   (E.J.-E.)

12. *Henry Irving responds to the word 'conscience'.* Craig was quite right about the freeze (although Craig actually refers to the moment when Irving first 'hears' the sleigh bells); he did freeze. But the hands crept up. He was buckling his right shoe and paused. And in that pause Irving used his face. You saw his face registering stark terror, anticipating his words of agreement, and with that thought his body slumped. Then a brief start, and he resumed his normal cheerfulness. But there was no rushing. He took time over it.   (E.J.-E.)

13. *Mathias's gift to Annette.* In both the manuscript version submitted to the Lord Chamberlain and in the early days of the first Lyceum performances, Mathias's gift is an Alsatian hat of the sort worn by married women (c.f. John Oxenford's review in *The Times*). The date when the hat was replaced by a necklace is unknown. When French's Acting Edition of the text was published, the substitution had not been made.   (D.M.).

My father, who first saw *The Bells* in 1880, told me that even then Irving's wedding gift to Annette was a gold necklace. And it wasn't contained in a basket, but in a small flat jeweller's case with a hinged lid and wrapped in paper.
                                                                                (E.J.-E.)

14. *Emendation to stage direction: Enter Sozel ...* Add to stage direction: (Sozel enters door R. with supper tray which she places on Table L. She then draws the window curtains and exits R.) This darkens the room still further and clears the backstage area for the setting of the vision prior to the sink and rise.
                                                                                (E.J.-E.)

15. *Mathias's response to 'Polish Jew's winter'.* Irving pretends to pick cork from his glass with his little finger, slowly saying 'Oh, you were talking about that, were you?' He then brushes his finger three times against his waistcoat and repeats, 'You were talking about that.' Irving took his time. It was all done with his face and eyes. You knew what he was thinking.   (E.J.-E.)

16. *Sleigh bells in Acts I and III.* 'As rehearsals for *The Bells* proceeded, the company became increasingly astonished by Irving's unorthodox approach to the play and by the decisive clarity with which he directed every inflexion and every piece of business in their parts and his own. Typical of this was the thought and care which he gave to the selection of suitable bells to represent the ghostly echo of the Jew's approaching sleigh. Having chosen the bells, which were mounted in a harness identical with that worn by sleigh horses, he insisted that the crescendo of their approach should be achieved realistically by the ringer starting from the back of the stage and continuing to jangle them until he reached the prompt corner, rather than arriving at the effect in the ordinary way by manipulating them from a fixed point' (Laurence Irving, *Henry Irving, The Actor and His World* (London, 1951), pp. 190–1).

82

17. *Mathias/Irving first hears the sleigh bells, probably from end of stage direction on page 47 (sleigh bells).* '... the whole torso of the man, also seeming frozen, was gradually, and by an almost perceptible movement, seen to be drawing up and back, as it would straighten a little, and to lean a little against the chair on which he was seated.

'Once in that position—motionless—eyes fixed ahead of him and fixed on us all—there he sat for the space of ten to twelve seconds which, I can assure you, seemed to us all like a lifetime, and then said—and said in a voice deep and overwhelmingly beautiful: "Oh, you were talking of that—were you?" And as the last syllable was uttered, there came from afar off the regular throbbing sound of sledge-bells.

'There he sat looking at us, and there sat the others, smoking and musing and comfortably motionless, except for the smoke from their pipes—and on and on went the sound of these bells, on and on and on—nothing else. Again, I assure you, that time seemed out of joint, and moved as it moves to us who suffer, when we wish it would move on and it does not stir.

'And the next step of his dance began' (Edward Gordon Craig, *Henry Irving*, pp. 59–60). We must regard this description with some caution, as it appears that Craig conflates this action with Irving's business earlier in the act when he removes his boots and draws on his shoes.   (D.M.)

18. *Mathias/Irving reacts to the sleigh-bells. Probably from stage direction mid-page 47: He looks at them ...* 'He moves his head slowly from us—the eyes still somehow with us—and moves it to the right—taking as long as a long journey to discover the truth takes. He looks to the faces on the right—nothing. Slowly the head revolves back again, down, and along the tunnels of thought and sorrow, and at the end the face and eyes are bent upon those to the left of him ... utter stillness ... nothing there either—every one is concerned with his or her little doings—smoking or knitting or unravelling wool or scraping a plate slowly and silently. A long pause, endless, breaking our hearts, comes down over everything, and on and on go these bells. Puzzled, motionless ... he glides up to a standing position: never has anyone seen another rising figure which slid slowly up like that. With one arm slightly raised, with sensitive hand speaking of far-off apprehended sounds, he asks, in the voice of some woman who is frightened, yet does not wish to frighten those with her: "Don't you ... don't you hear the sound of sledge-bells on the road?" "Sledge-bells?" grumbles the smoking man; "Sledge-bells?" pipes his companion; "Sledge-bells?" says the wife—all of them seemingly too sleepy and comfortable to apprehend anything ... see anything ... or understand ... and, as they grumble a negative, suddenly he staggers and shivers from his toes to his neck; his jaws begin to chatter; the hair on his forehead, falling over, writhes as though it were a nest of little snakes. Everyone is on his feet at once to help: "Caught a chill" ... "let's get him to bed" ... and *one* of the moments of the immense and touching dance closes' (Edward Gordon Craig, *Henry Irving*, pp. 59–60).

A few comments on Craig's recollections' (1) Mathias was the only one eating, and he certainly wasn't scraping his plate! (2) In neither Irving's production when I saw it nor in H.B.'s revival did Catherine respond to Mathias's query about hearing sleigh-bells. (3) The line 'Let's get him to bed' was never heard by my father nor by me.   (E.J.-E.)

19. *Tuned sleigh bells.* '... Irving was, in the character of a manager, not a whit less thoughtful, less careful, of every detail that helped to make the whole of a play ... It was in his dressing-room ... that several sets of new sledge-bells attached to miniature collars were brought to him. One of them was to be used in a coming revival of the piece which had made him famous. He had them sounded in succession, with a well-managed indication of the close, distant, and graduated effects, over and over again, while he listened intently before he began to eliminate them one by one until one set was left for final consideration. Then he listened more carefully than ever to that set, and then he turned to Mr. Loveday, a very accomplished musician, and said, "Now isn't that the right set?" a question which produced an emphatic "Not a doubt about it." Details of this kind may at first mention seem mere trifles; yet it was the minute attention given to them that produced the then singular homogeneousness that marked all performances given at the Lyceum' (W. H. Pollock, *Impressions*, pp. 6–7).

20. *Irving responds to the clock striking 10.* The bells have been jingling since the mention of the 'Polish Jew's winter', but now, alone, the bells are at first the only sound. Then the music enters diminuendo, with the clock chiming before striking the hour. He listens. He stops, standing just looking at the audience. And you can tell by his face what's happening, Irving's sudden movements and his words following after his thoughts.

  Both Henry Irving and H.B. varied the pace through this tense scene. Terror was the keynote.

  When Mathias falls with a prolonged cry, the Coda is played by the orchestra as the Curtain descends on Act One.   (E.J.-E.)

21. *Original scenery for* The Bells *sink and rise for vision.* Unpacking scenery in America for first tour (1883–4) produced litter of screws and other evidence of cumbersome packing. According to Stoker, 'When I came down to the theatre on the first loading of the stuff, Arnott, who was in charge of the mechanics of the stage came to me and said:

  '"Would you mind coming here a moment, sir, I would like you to see something!" He brought me to the back of the stage and pointed out a long heap of rubbish some four feet high. It was just such as you would see in the waste-heap of a house-wrecker's yard.

  '"What on earth is that?" I asked.

  '"That is the sink-and-rise of the vision in *The Bells*."

  'In effecting a vision on the stage the old method used to be to draw the back scenes or "flats" apart or else raise the whole scene from above or take it down through a long trap on the stage. The latter was the method adopted by the scene-painter of *The Bells*.

  '"Did it meet with an accident?" I asked.

'"No, sir. It simply shook to bits just as you see it. It was packed up secure and screwed tight like the rest!"

'I examined it carefully. The whole stuff was simply rotten with age and wear; as thoroughly worn out as the deacon's wonderful one-horse shay in Oliver Wendell Holmes's poem. The canvas had been almost held together by the overlay of paint, and as for the wood it was cut and hacked and pieced to death; full of old screw-holes and nail-holes. No part of it had been of new timber or canvas when *The Bells* was produced eleven years before. With this experience I examined the whole scenery and found that almost every piece of it was in a similar condition. It had been manufactured out of all the odds and ends of old scenery in the theatre' (Bram Stoker, *Personal Reminiscences of Henry Irving*, vol. I (London, 1906), pp. 142–3).

Property horse in the 'vision scene'. '... Arnott, the Property Master and a fine workman, had an odd experience during the Bristol week. Something had gone wrong with the travelling "property" horse used in the vision scene ..., and he had come up to town to bring the real one from storage. In touring it was usual to bring a "profile" representation of the gallant steed. "Profile" has in theatrical parlance a special meaning other than the dictionary meaning of an "outline". It is thin wood covered on both sides with rough canvas carefully glued down. It is very strong and can be cut in safety to any shape. The profile horse was of course an outline, but the art of the scene-painter had rounded it out to seemingly natural dimensions. Now the "real" horse, though a lifeless "property", had in fact been originally alive. It was formed of the skin of a moderately sized pony; and being embellished with picturesque attachments in the shape of mane and tail was a really creditable object. But it was expensive to carry as it took up much space. Arnott and two of his men ran up to fetch this down as there was not time to make a new profile horse. When they got to Paddington he found that the authorities refused to carry the goods by weight on account of its bulk, and asked him something like £4 for the journey. He expressed his feelings feely, as men occasionally do under irritating circumstances, and said he would go somewhere else. The clerk in the office smiled and Arnott went away; he was a clever man who did not like to be beaten, and railways were his natural enemies. He thought the matter over. Having looked over the timetable and found that the cost of a horse-box to Bristol was only £1.13s., he went to the department in charge of such matters and ordered one, paying for it at once and arranging that it should go on the next fast train. By some manoeuvring he so managed that he and his men took Koveski's horse into the box and closed the doors.

'When the train arrived at Bristol there had to be some shunting to and fro so as to place the horsebox in the siding arranged for such matters. The officials in charge threw open the door for the horse to walk out. But he would yield to no blandishment, nor even to the violence of chastisement usual at such times. A little time passed and the officials got anxious, for the siding was required for other purposes. The station at Bristol is not roomy and more than one line has to use it. The official in charge told him to take out his damned horse!

'"Not me!" said he, for he was now seeing his way to "get back" at the railway company, "I've paid for the carriage of the horse and I want him delivered out of your premises. The rate I paid includes the services of the necessary officials."

'The porters tried again, but the horse would not stir. Now it is a dangerous matter to go into a horsebox in case the horse should prove restive. One after another the porters declined, till at last one plucky lad volunteered to go in by the little window close to the horse's head. Those on the platform waited in apprehension, till he suddenly ran out of the box laughing and crying out: "Why you blamed fools. He ain't a 'orse at all. He's a stuffed 'un!"' (Bram Stoker, *Personal Reminiscences of Henry Irving*, vol. I (London, 1906), pp. 63–5).

Light in the forge . . . end of Act I . . . Royal Command performance at Sandringham 1889. 'Those who saw Irving in *The Bells* . . . will remember perhaps in that vision at the end of Act I a tiny light is seen in the distant snow-covered landscape. Irving, as his imagination pictures it in the dream scene says: "and old Franz' forge—how brightly it glows upon the hillock." I was the forge'. The tiny light which represented Franz' forge had to be held behind the backcloth; there were barely nine inches between the backcloth and the wall, and as I was the thinnest man in the company I had been chosen for this duty' (*The Autobiography of Sir John Martin-Harvey*, p. 119).

Actor playing the Jew. Vision scene. The actor playing the Jew stands in the sleigh driving his horse. Slowly he turns his face downstage towards Mathias and stares at him.

Irving double. 'Charles Thomas Hunt Helmsley . . . one of the "Lyceum gentlemen" . . . his tall figure recommended him to Irving as suitable to appear as his "double" in plays like *The Bells* . . . In the case of *The Bells* this "double" would represent "Mathias" in the vision which brought down the curtain on the first act" (*The Autobiography of Sir John Martin-Harvey*, pp. 75–6). Helmsley married Martin-Harvey's sister, May, in 1888. He later became stage-manager to Sir George Alexander at the St James's Theatre and remained with him for twenty years. (E.J.-E.)

22. *Irving strengthened ending of act.* Irving altered Lewis's ending to the act. Originally Mathias was not alone, but was accompanied by Catherine in the vision scene. In the Lord Chamberlain's manuscript copy, the text is as follows:

MATHIAS. The Jew is dead. He cannot return. It is the wine and cold that have overcome me.

Vision of the Jew's murder

MATHIAS. Ha! Great Heaven! It is the Jew. Though he be dead. Ha!

CATHERINE. What ails you Mathias! What are you glaring at so strangely? You are ill. Oh! Help! Help!

Curtain. (D.M.)

86

ACT II

1. *Hawes Craven backcloth to Act II.* This (reproduced on page 95), although identified with *The Bells*, raises some doubts. It shows not an Alsatian village, but a town. It was used in the 1882 production of J. R. Planché's *The Captain of the Watch* and may have been used in Lyceum and touring productions of *The Bells.* It was lost in the fire of 1897, which destroyed the Lyceum's scenic stores in Bear Lane, Southwark. However, there is some conflicting evidence on this matter. According to Brereton, 'The scenery for *The Bells* and *The Merchant of Venice* was at the Lyceum and so escaped destruction' (*Life of Henry Irving*, vol. 2, p. 271). Whereas according to Stoker '... the scenery for *The Bells* and *The Captain of the Watch* and *The Merchant of Venice* were all in the store and destroyed ... When for repertoire purposes in later years several [sets of scenery] were required, *Louis XI, Charles I, The Bells, The Lyons Mail, Olivia, Faust, Becket* were all reproduced at an aggregate cost of over eleven thousand pounds' (*Personal Reminiscences of Henry Irving*, p. 426).
(D.M.)

When I saw *The Bells* in February 1905 the backcloth for the second act depicted a snow-covered village street. It was certainly *not* the backcloth by Hawes Craven. (E.J.-E.)

2. *Irving's change to start of Act II.* Irving changed Lewis's beginning to Act II, which in the manuscript version opens with Mathias alone, speaking his determination 'to sleep alone, lest talk betray me.' (D.M.)

3. *Mathias's scene with Annette.* In every scene with Annette both Henry Irving and H.B. displayed exquisite tenderness. The relationship between father and daughter was very close and mutual. Never for a moment would one suspect that Mathias was capable of committing a brutal murder. (E.J.-E.)

4. This most important stage direction should read:
> MATHIAS, *left alone, sighs, rises and walks to door L. then up to window C.* VILLAGERS, MEN *and* WOMEN *in Sunday clothes, pass by in couples.* ANNETTE *and* CATHERINE *pass and kiss hands to him. He returns the compliment. A woman in the group says, 'Good Morning, Burgomaster!'*
> *The church bell stops ringing.*
> MATH. *(coming down C. to L. of table R.C.):* Everything goes well. *(He takes snuff box and taps it forcibly)* But what a lesson, Mathias ... etc.

Sozel does not appear at all. She is in the kitchen from whence she is later summoned by Mathias. (E.J.-E.)

5. *Tempo of soliloquy.* There is a continual change of tempo—like driving a coach and horses: now whipping up, now pulling in, continuously varying the pace. This is an actor's play, not a director's. (E.J.-E.)

6. *Counting out Annette's dowry.* Mathias empties a large leather bag on to the table, pouring out gold coins and rouleaux (stacks of coins tightly wrapped in stiff paper cylinders). About a hundred Louis d'or are loose. You'll notice

that when he counts out the coins, he thrice reaches the number thirteen. That touch is Irving's, not in Lewis's text. Superstitious actors following Irving have omitted or altered the count. (E.J.-E.)

7. Irving referred to the Jew's money belt as 'belt', not 'girdle'. (E.J.-E.)

8. '... *in a blacksmith's shop, hid under some old iron.*' Replace *hid* with *hidden*. (E.J.-E.)

9. *Mathias.* 'Not *like that* ...' Irving later changed this speech to read 'The fools!—not to destroy all evidence against them. To be hanged through the blade of an old knife. Not like that—not like that—(wiping the sweat from his neck) am *I* to be caught!' (D.M.)

10. *Christian taps at window C.* Christian passes at the back, stops at C. window and taps upon it. Mathias looks round with a start. Seeing who it is he murmurs 'Ah, Christian!' then, going to the table R.C. he replaces the rouleaux and coins in the bag. He is locking them in the escritoire as Christian enters. Irving deleted the music provided for this action. (E.J.-E.)

11. *Stove in Act II.* The stove door is hinged on its upstage side so that when it is opened the light from the fire within (red and amber glass mediums) is thrown downstage upon Mathias as he opens the door. The bright sunshine in the street outside was obtained with floods with light amber glass mediums focused on the snow cloth. The only interior darkness comes from the dark oak panelling. When electric lighting was used, electricians were instructed to dim the daylight to emphasise Irving's face. Henry Irving's face in the red glow from the open stove is a vivid memory. And so is H.B.'s. (E.J.-E.)

12. *Picking up coke.* Irving opens the stove door with the tongs, he picks up a lump of coke and feeds it into the fire. He quickly drops a second lump of coke then, seconds later, drops the tongs with a loud clatter. (E.J.-E.)

13. *Dropping tongs.* After Irving dropped fire tongs, he then mopped his forehead with a blue-grey handkerchief. (E.J.-E.)

The business of Mathias dropping the tongs was so memorable a part of *The Bells* as to be imitated and parodied. In George and Weedon Grossmith's *The Diary of a Nobody* (1892) Mr Burwin-Fosselton, who bores everyone with his imitations of Irving, quoted scraps of plays and 'more than once knocked over the fire-irons, making a hideous row' (Chapter XI). (D.M.)

14. *Stage direction.* Rather than 'springing at Christian, etc.', Irving modified this direction. It should now read (*laughing hysterically, and slapping Christian on shoulders, face and arms*). When George Alexander played Christian in the 1884 production, Irving had the habit of slapping so heartily that Alexander was quite bruised. Seeking Ellen Terry's advice, Alexander was advised to hit back on the line 'You—you Burgomaster, ha ha.' Alexander followed her advice, and an astonished Irving thereafter slapped with less force. (E.J.-E.)

15. *Irving's laugh/Mathias's scene with Christian.* '... I do not know, and cannot guess, how many times I have seen this particular play, but every time I saw

it, up to [Irving's] last appearances as Mathias in London, I found in it one of many instances of a thing which was characteristic of him ... This thing was that he never rested content with what he had accomplished. He never docketed a part as completed from his own view: on the contrary, he never rested from trying to improve, and again improve, and still always improve on his rendering ... This was markedly the case with ... Mathias in *The Bells*; but here, as elsewhere, the constant process of improvement inevitably involved the rejection or change of certain effects that one was sorry to miss. One such effect I found in the laugh with which Mathias interrupts his son-in-law to be, Christian, the captain of gendarmes, in expounding a theory which shows him to be perilously close on the truth as to the murder of the Jew. The laugh in question broke in upon, one might say was part of, the burgomaster's speech interrupting the gendarme's analysis of the crime. "Take care, Christian, take care! I—I myself had a lime-kiln at the time!" In the first performances of the play the "take care" seemed wrung from Mathias by the deadly logic of Christian's theory that the Jew's body was consumed in a lime-kiln; while the nervous system strained to breaking-point than of an attempt to cover up the impulse of a startled mind and conscience. The effect was thrilling, as I think all who remember it will acknowledge.

'In later representations the whole speech, save for a touch maybe in the two opening words, seemed due to a continued habit of caution and calculation, while the laugh rang hard, dull, mechanical. The latter rendering was undoubtedly the more artistic, as a little reflection on a point to which the actor had doubtless given a good deal will show. For the key to the whole of Mathias's outward life since the murder of the Jew is found in an unremitting preparedness for such a blow as Christian's reasoned reconstitution of the crime, an unceasing repression in all company, even that of his wife alone, of his inward emotions, a watchfulness that never relaxed lest by word, look, or action he should betray something which would lead to his own undoing. Therefore the later interpretation was the right one, though it produced a lesser immediate effect' Walter Herries Pollock, *Impressions of Henry Irving* (London, 1908), pp. 3–6).

16. *Mathias jokes with Christian and Annette.* This little interlude is played lightly and jocularly. There is no trace of the hysterical jarring laughter to which Mathias gives vent when, earlier, Christian mentions the lime-kiln. The ensuing scene with his wife, Catherine, is likewise played tenderly and with great feeling. (E.J.-E.)

17. Following the stage directions (*Taking snuff. Places snuff box on table*), the next stage direction should begin: *Enter* NOTARY, CLERK, SOZEL, *and* FOUR GIRLS with floral bouquets. MATHIAS *greets them....* The rest of the direction is correct. (E.J.-E.)

18. *Business of reading contract.* The villagers enter, the girls carrying nosegays, the men bearing and wearing crimson and white wedding favours. The musicians, playing the Lauterbach enter and go upstage right. The villagers chatter

to one another, point to Annette, comment on her appearance. The notary mimes the business of reading the contract aloud, but his words cannot be heard above the music. The notary's clerk was dropped from the production to simplify the stage business at this point. (D.M.)

19. *Villagers*. The villagers and all other non-speaking roles were performed by trained supernumeraries. Even on the farewell tour in 1905 such large numbers were needed for *Becket* and *The Lyons Mail* that Irving brought a full company with him. Martin-Harvey, however, took on local supernumeraries for his tours of *The Bells*. (E.J.-E.)

20. *Betrothal scene*. Mathias's reaction to Walter's "digging him in the ribs" is to assume that Walter intends to stop the contract and he, Mathias, registers apprehension. (E.J.-E.)

21. *Song of the Betrothal—known as 'The Lauterbach'*. Following Father Walter's request, Annette, holding Christian by the hand, shyly steps forward to centre stage and sings the first verse. She then joins in the Tyrolienne with Christian as her partner. At the conclusion of the valse, she again leads Christian to centre stage and sings the second verse. This is followed by a repetition of the Tyrolienne valse—the stage being filled with swirling, revelling villagers, some dancers waltzing in the routine style, others adopting the Alsatian fashion of placing their hands on each other's shoulders and twirling round. The scene is one of gaiety, noise, and colour. When the valse is at its height, Mathias again 'hears' the sleigh bells. He throws his arms in the air and, shouting 'the Bells! the Bells!', he rushes amidst the dancers. Catherine, thoroughly alarmed, follows him. Mathias seizes her by the waist and waltzes madly round and round crying 'Ring on! Ring on!' The curtain descends rapidly. Irving amended the final line to 'Ring on! Ring on—to Hell!' (E.J.-E.)

22. *Tyrolienne section of music*. In Irving's production there was no singing in this section, just general gaiety and laughter. (E.J.-E.)
 The 'valse chantée' in the Paris 1869 version is the 'Lauterbach'. (D.M.)

23. *Village musicians for betrothal scene*. Irving's onstage musicians were 2–3 violinists, percussion and a double bass player. That was until 1885 according to my father. After that the music was played off L. It was when I saw the play at Boscombe. (E.J.-E.)

ACT III

1. *Stage direction, Act III opening*. Sozel enters carrying both the lighted candle with its extinguisher and a carafe of water, with a glass inverted over its neck. She places these on the bedside table right, then goes up right to pick up the chair which she places left of the table. Sozel stands aside as Mathias, Catherine, Father Walter and Hans enter. The latter two are amusingly drunk. Their business is played for laughs. (E.J.-E.)

2. *Irving's change to start of Act III*. Lewis's manuscript version begins with Mathias already alone. The long series of goodnights has been added by Irving

to establish the love Mathias holds for his family and friends and their anxiety for him. (D.M.)

3. *Violin solo.* The violin solo does not appear in the score. The direction calling for his music apparently is a stage-managerial jotting which was never realised. (D.M.)

4. *Music direction.* Another stage-managerial note not followed in performance. There is nothing in the score to indicate that the betrothal chorus was played here, nor is there time to play it before Music cue 11 is given. (D.M.)

5. *Stage direction.* On tour the roles of Karl and Tony were dropped and all business and lines were performed by Fritz. (E.J.-E.)

6. *Irving's reading.* I do not recall Irving exclaiming 'I never dream!' fiercely. It was said with weary emphasis and with a faraway look in his eyes. (E.J.-E.)

7. *Stage direction (locking door).* Mathias listens to Catherine's and Annette's retreating footsteps, rises and crosses to the door left, pauses there, opens the door a little way and peeps through to see that they have truly gone, closes the door quietly, then locks it with a firm motion, the lock turning with an audible click as he turns the key, then returns slowly to the chair. (E.J.-E.)

8. *Mathias having divested himself of his coat and vest.* Having drunk the water, Mathias takes out his watch and chatelaine from the right fob of his knee breeches, winds it, then places it on the bedside table. He then casually removes his coat and waistcoat while speaking his lines and lays them on the back of the chair. The business is played over the laughter and singing from the street below. (E.J.-E.)

9. *Stage direction: Mathias's arm is seen* ... The arm belongs to another actor. Irving has gone to prepare for the dream scene. In the first production his double was J. H. Barnes who also doubled as Mathias in the vision scenes ending Act I. (D.M.)

10. *Dream scene.* 'Of the dream scene it is sufficient to say that Irving's astounding power made one forgive its outrageous length. It was rendered impressive, not by trick and artifice, but by sheer acting power' (Charles Hiatt, *Henry Irving, A Record and Review* (London, 1903), p. 102).

11. *J. Martin-Harvey onstage with Irving (1883).* '... for the most part I was still inarticulate; as ... an Alsatian peasant and juryman in *The Bells* the last was a thrilling experience, Seated in the semi-darkness of the Hall in the Court House I watched Irving, within a few feet of him, go through the agony of his dream and once again, under the spell of the mesmerist, experience all the horror of that night when he murdered the Polish Jew. It was a marvellous opportunity for studying his every movement and noting every cadence of his voice. I see the alabaster-like outline of his face cutting clear across the gloom of the Hall; I see his frantic efforts to resist the skill of the mesmerist. When at last Mathias succumbs, and the day of the murder is "suggested" to him, I hear the long-drawn somnambulistic sigh as he answers—"Yes?" Again, when

(living through the scene in trance) he has decided to kill the Jew, and pauses outside his house, in the silence of the snow, waiting and listening for his victim, I listen to the pathetic cadence of his voice as Mathias hears the distant wail of his little daughter—"Little Annette is crying." I hear the cry of relief when the church clock beats midnight and, believing that the Jew has already passed, and that he has been saved from the crime of murder, he sinks upon his knees in a passion of gratitude—"Thank God! Thank God!" I hear his horrified scream as he forces himself to look at his dead victim and recoils in terror from the fixed stare of the Jew's dead eyes. Every moment is burnt into my remembrance and I could still describe each moment of that masterly scene. How long it was to be before I could put into practice the glorious lessons it was my privilege to receive! Lessons which were, nevertheless, stowed away in my subconscious for use in due season' (*The Autobiography of Sir John Martin-Harvey* (London, 1932), pp. 74–5).

12. *Gauze in the Dream scene*. 'I remember ... at Columbus, Ohio, when Irving was playing the Dream Scene in *The Bells*. The gauze, behind which he enacted the hypnotic movements of "Mathias" while under the influence of the mesmerist, became detached from its batten and hung like a cobweb across the stage in such a way as to conceal all Irving did on that portion of the scene. Irving, without coming out of the character of the dream-haunted "Mathias", deliberately tore down the remaining portion of the huge gauze which was left hanging across the Proscenium opening and played the remainder of the scene to all the usual enthusiasm' (*The Autobiography of Sir John Martin-Harvey*, p. 128).

13. *Stage direction*. Everything happens in perfect silence. The actors, treading on a tick canvas stagecloth, wear soft-soled shoes and make no sound when moving in this dream sequence.   (E.J.-E.)

14. *Appearance of the court*. The panelling of Mathias's bedchamber is painted on gauze, behind which a black backing is hung. In the darkness the black backing is flown to enable the court to appear as if in a bluish grey haze, the haze being created by the gauze. Behind the gauze steel blue limelights from the O.P. flies pick out and follow Mathias throughout the scene. The other characters are in shadow or in reflected light. Clement Scott describes the court's frescoes, but these were not clearly visible. He must have seen them backstage.

Lighting for the Dream scene. We know from the original lighting plot in the script that the fly limes had iris diaphragms controlled by the operator. These, when used correctly, provided the essential dream-like quality of the lighting. There were never any sharply defined circles of light; nor could figures be clearly distinguished as regards exact details of costumes. One knew there were three Judges, a Clerk of the Court, barristers, members of the public, and uniformed gendarmes (see the Charles Buchel drawing made in 1902). But the whole effect was hazy and like a dream. Even Mathias was a figure with a dream-like, insubstantial and almost spectral appearance; though his facial expressions could be clearly seen.

With the general introduction of electric lighting, 'frosts' were added to the mediums in the fly focus lights. These, plus the iris diaphragms, provided a similar effect when—from 1909 onwards—the play was revived by H. B. Irving, Edward Dunstan, Henry Baynton, and the others I have mentioned. But on Baynton's first night at the Savoy in 1924, the lighting was far too bright. This may have been due to back-stage electrical staff changes, and the rapid 'get-in' at the week-end. Whatever the cause, it was regrettable and Baynton had my sincere sympathy. (E.J.-E.)

15. *Mesmerist.* 'This was Jack Archer; the "Mesmerist" in *The Bells* (very wooden) ...' (*The Autobiography of Sir John Martin-Harvey*, p. 58).

16. *Mesmerist in Lewis's ms.* In Lewis's manuscript the Mesmerist is called the 'Clairvoyant'. (D.M.)

17. In response to the President's query 'Can you send this man to sleep?' and the Mesmerist's reply, 'I can', Mathias backs away, the steel blue limelight falling upon his face. Mathias resists the Mesmerist, but all the audience sees clearly is Mathias's face and the white undulating hands of the Mesmerist who stands behind him. Mathias throws back the hood of the blouse when commencing his very first speech in the dream sequence. (E.J.-E.)

18. *'I will not sleep.'* Irving repeats 'I will not sleep' many times, taking a long while to resist the Mesmerist. With each repetition of the phrase, his words are slower, more broken by pauses. He takes his time over this scene. (E.J.E.)

19. *Mathias's 'He looks at me—he has grey eyes.'* Irving added here, 'I'll do it.' (E.J.-E.)

20. *Irving's pronunciation ... trial scene.* 'Again, when in the same dream he spoke the line: "How the dogs howl at Daniel's farm—how they how-ow-ow-l-l-l," it had to be admitted that we never said it like that—I must confess that it can only once be said so, and by one man only, and in this very scene' (E. G. Craig, *Henry Irving*, p. 63).

21. *Irving's pronunciation ... trial scene.* 'It was brought out against Irving that he could not speak our English tongue ... He would say ... "*Ritz*" for "*Rich*". This word *rich* spoken as *ritz—ritz—ritz—ritz* he repeated, as some will remember, where he imagines he is in a field and awaiting the coming of the Polish Jew, and hears the bells of his sledge afar off, coming nearer and nearer. The effect of the *ritz* for *rich* was this: instead of the sound reminding us of an old housewife shooing the fowls away from the kitchen door, we were horribly thrilled, as at the ominous sound of the serpent about to strike, and we were aware that a duet between the regular throb of the bells and this voice was being sung. At the end of a long sustained series of these sounds, he sprang—he struck down the imaginary Jew and fell in a heap on top of him' (E. G. Craig, *Henry Irving*, pp. 62–3).

22. *Sir John Martin-Harvey's approach to the final scene.* 'At the end of the Court scene I take it that the clash of wedding bells is heard during the change.

Immediately voices should be heard as from below, and through the sounds "MATHIAS, *where is* MATHIAS? *The bride is waiting*" coming quickly nearer and nearer up the stairs. At the moment that the front scene comes into view, the voices should have reached the door. One voice—Madame Mathias—and another (the best voice you have) should call out—"MATHIAS, MATHIAS, *the bride's waiting*" and simultaneously MATHIAS should appear at the same moment with KATHARINE [*sic*], CHRISTIAN, ANNETTE and which ever others you think advisable, come on the stage from the other side. This would form a picture for a second, paralysing the group with terror and rooting them to the spot as MATHIAS says *"Take the rope from my neck. Take the rope from my neck"*. Immediately KATHARINE, CHRISTIAN and ANNETTE move down stage, MADAM MATHIAS, as before, helping MATHIAS to his chair.

This will take hardly a minute and will cut out the unnecessary cross of CHRISTIAN, which was always a bad moment.

ANNETTE and CHRISTIAN will take up the positions they are in until the end of the play.

Each person who speaks must have a definite line, but the definite lines must be spoken together and it will be MADAME MATHIAS, and not CHRISTIAN, who first enters the room.

These lines should be spoken—(From below)

MAN   Burgomaster, Burgomaster, the bride's waiting.

KATHARINE   Mathias, Mathias, our guests are waiting below.

MAN'S VOICE   Do you wonder he is sleeping soundly, *after the wine last night?*

> *By this time they are on the stairs and* KATHARINE *is at the door. She calls up the stairs as she is coming along:*

Mathias, Mathias, my dear, come along: have you forgotten it is the wedding day?

> *By the time she says this she has opened the door and is facing Mathias. This must be timed and rehearsed very carefully, as every moment saved is of value.*
>
> *The noise of coming up stairs should not be loud as it is a tiresome sound for the audience and distracts them.*

(CURTAIN *and* LINES, *as before*)

(From notes made by Martin-Harvey for his 1932 revival of *The Bells*. Lent by E.J.-E. to the Russell-Cotes Museum.)

Sir John Martin-Harvey's reconstruction of the last scene of Act Three of The Bells. How can Madame Mathias open the door? Mathias locked it before going to bed. The original scene as played by Henry Irving and the others (including myself) with Christian breaking down the door is far more dramatic. Christian's cross to the alcove and pulling back the curtain sustained the suspense. How could Harvey describe it as 'Always a bad moment?' In my experience it never seemed to be.   (E.J.-E.)

23. *Irving's end to Act III.* Irving held centre stage at the play's end, lengthening his part by adding his dying words against the diminishing peals of the marriage bells and by striking from Lewis's script Walter's (and the play's) final line,

'Be comforted. He was a noble fellow, while he lived—and he has died without pain.' (D.M.)

Irving's pronunciation . . . Act III . . . final line of play. He would say . . . '*Tak the rup frum mey nek*' for '*Take the rope from my neck*' (E. G. Craig, *Henry Irving*, p. 62).

'*Take the rope from my neck—take—the rope—neck.*' Henry Irving did not say that when I saw him. He gasped out the words, 'The rope! [pause] The rope!—choking gasp—Cut—the—rope . . . from me nek!' We then heard a long-drawn-out sigh as the body of Mathias (after the death struggle) slumped in the chair, and the curtain fell. There was a considerable pause before the hypnotised audience realised that the play had ended and commenced to applaud tumultuously. My father told me that Irving often altered the final words in the death scene. He also used to vary the ending of *Louis XI.* According-ing to my father, Irving's greatness as an actor lay in the fact that he was always striving to improve his interpretation of the character he was playing. But he strictly reserved any variation to scenes where he was the sole actor. He was a stickler for giving and receiving the exact cues. (E.J.-E.)

Backcloth by Hawes Craven, thought by some scholars to have been used in Act II. See note 1, page 87.

95

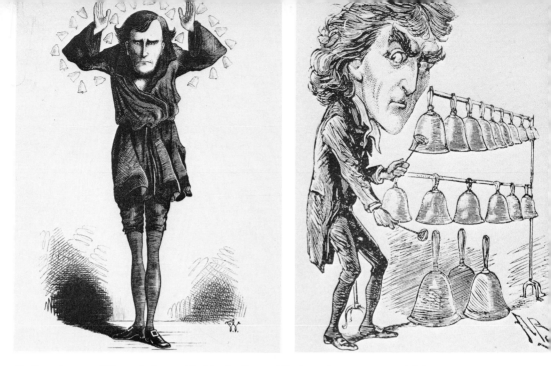

(*Left*) caricature of Henry Irving as Mathias in *Once a Week*, 13 January 1872; (*right*) caricature of Henry Irving, commemorating the twenty-fifth anniversary of *The Bells*, by Alfred Bryan in *The Entr'acte*, 5 December 1896.

(*Below and opposite page, above*) testimonial signed and presented by Irving's associates at the Lyceum Theatre on 25 November 1892 to commemorate the twenty-first anniversary of *The Bells*.

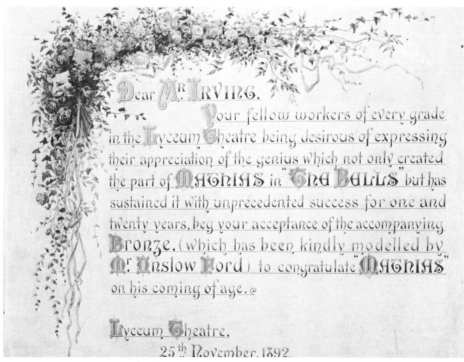

Dear Mr IRVING,

Your fellow workers of every grade in the Lyceum Theatre being desirous of expressing their appreciation of the genius which not only created the part of MATHIAS in "THE BELLS" but has sustained it with unprecedented success for one and twenty years, beg your acceptance of the accompanying Bronze, (which has been kindly modelled by Mr Onslow Ford) to congratulate "MATHIAS" on his coming of age.

Lyceum Theatre,
25th November. 1892.

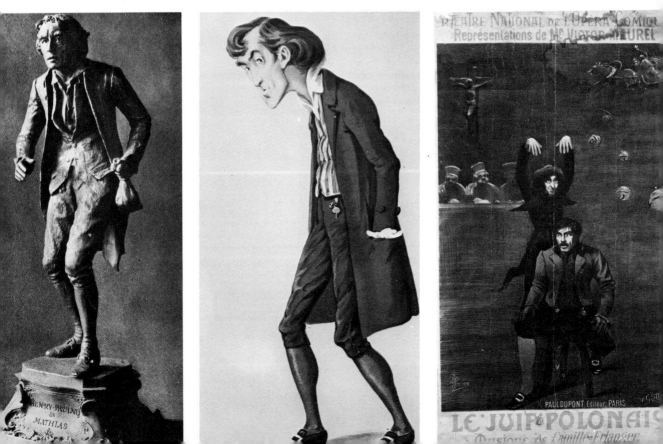

(*Left*) statuette of Henry Irving as Mathias by E. Onslow Ford, R. A., presented to Irving on 25 November 1872 to commemorate the twenty-first anniversary of *The Bells*; (*middle*) caricature of Henry Irving as Mathias by 'Ape' in *Vanity Fair*, 19 December 1874; and (*right*) poster for an operatic adaptation of *Le Juif Polonais* by at the Opéra Comique, Paris, 1897.

H. B. Irving as Mathias, from the poster for his revival of the play at the Queen's Theatre, 22 September 1909.

(*Left*) H. B. Irving as Mathias in the 'dream scene' in the 1909 production of *The Bells*; (*middle*) Henry Baynton; and (*right*) Sir John Martin-Harvey as Mathias.

Bransby Williams as Mathias in the 1950 B.B.C. television production of *The Bells*.

(*Left*) Bransby Williams as Mathias; (*middle*) Eric Jones-Evans as Mathias; and (*right*) Eric Jones-Evans.

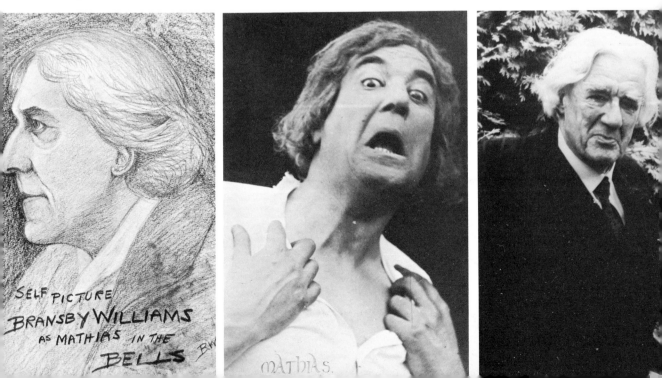

REVIEWS OF *THE BELLS*

CLEMENT SCOTT IN *THE OBSERVER*, SUNDAY 26 NOVEMBER 1871

We have so recently sketched the literary and dramatic history of that extraordinary psychological study, 'Le Juif Polonais,' by M.M. Erckmann-Chatrian, on the occasion of the production of Mr. Burnand's version, called 'Paul Zegers', at the Alfred Theatre, that it only becomes necessary to note the different treatment by Mr. Leopold Lewis, in his drama of 'The Bells', which was received on its first production with the most gratifying enthusiasm. We have before remarked upon the fact that the weird story, though written in dramatic form, was not originally intended for stage representation, and have given our opinion that, without picturesque scenery and detail, coupled with powerful acting, the study is comparatively worthless for histrionic purposes. Mr. Burnand departed widely from the authors' intention, and by adding a prologue and toning down many of the terrible details, gave us more of a stage play, and much less of a psychological study. Mr. Leopold Lewis, on the other hand, has more faithfully followed the lead of the authors, has preserved the poetical pictures of Alsatian life, and, with one conspicuous and most important exception, gives us the idea of M.M. Erckmann-Chatrian. The exception in question must be recognised, because, as it seems to us, Mr. Lewis has, for the sake of a beautiful stage picture, sacrificed the most important dramatic point in the tale. We take it the intention of the authors was to represent the outward and inner life of a man whose conscience is burdened with the hideous weight of a murder committed fifteen years ago—of a crime, by means of which he obtained capital, success, and the best prizes the world can bestow. The fact of the murder having been committed by Mathias, the respected burgomaster, is only to be suggested to the audience by his uneasiness and trouble when alone. In society he is to be the most genial and charming of men; in private he is to be torn with an agony of grief. The first act is artistically contrived to show this double life.

The scene is Christmas Eve, an occasion consecrated to domesticity. Though the snow is deep and blinding without, the hearth of the burgomaster is bright, and sorrow is unknown in the happy household. The wife is anxiously awaiting her lord's return; the daughter, happy in the love of a young and honourable man, has still a warm corner in her heart for the father she idolises. In comes

Mathias from the cold, apparently the picture of health and happiness. He brings with him kisses for his wife, and a bridal present for the pretty daughter. He sits down to his supper as hungry as a hunter, and the first glass is raised to his lips to toast his family and his friends, when an accidental remark of one of the guests recalls the murder of a Polish Jew, who on this very night, at this very hour, started from this very inn, fifteen years ago, and was never seen again. The wine-cup is put down untasted, and for an instant a cloud comes over the happy face of Mathias. It is well to notice how the dramatic interest increases. Suddenly a noise of bells is heard across the snow, a sledge stops at the door, a man in Polish costume stands on the threshold, asking a blessing on the assembled family, and craving hospitality. Mathias, horrified at this terrible coincidence—for, of course, it is nothing but a coincidence; it is not the murdered Jew, nor the murdered Jew's brother, but merely a chance visit of another wanderer, similarly apparelled to the inn—falls down in a fit, and the act concludes with the cry, 'Le médecin! courez chercher le médecin!' Strange to say, this double Jew has been objected to by those who most admire and appreciate the story. 'Who is he? and what is he?' they say, failing to see that he is merely introduced in order to re-enact, by a strange fatality, the same scene of fifteen years ago.

Be that as it may, Mr. Leopold Lewis has dismissed the second Jew; he has omitted the original termination of the act; he has given a wrench to the quietly revolving wheels of the story, and he supplies, instead of the tragic incident, a picture of the actual murder supposed to be seen by Mathias during his delirium. The illusion is admirably contrived, and most effective. It called down shouts of applause from the audience; but it has just this ill effect, it tells the listeners unhesitatingly that Mathias is a murderer, and this is scarcely what M.M. Erckmann-Chatrian desired to do at this moment. It is only in this instance Mr. Lewis departs from the French play in any important manner, though we own we could have wished the concluding lines of the original drama could have been preserved, which show that, in spite of all, the Alsatian family are unshaken in their confidence in the beloved burgomaster. The death of Mathias is ascribed by the kindly old doctor to the poor fellow's habit of drinking too much white wine. His family believe him to be an honest, upright fellow to the last.

We have before commented upon the extraordinary difficulty attending the proper representation of the character of Mathias, the murderer, particularly in the overlong dream scene, in which the guilty man is brought before his judges, and under mesmeric influences, re-enacts the murder. It must be unanimously granted that Mr. Henry Irving's performance is most striking, and cannot fail to make an impression. There are possibly very few who were aware that this actor possessed so much undeveloped power, and would be capable in such a character, of succeeding so well. His notion of the haunted man is conceived with great cleverness, and though, here and there, there are apparent faults, there are points of detail which are really admirable. The study, to begin with, is one eminently picturesque. Mr. Irving was never less mannered. The two most striking points in the performance are the powerful acting as the poor frenzied creature dozes off at the will of the mesmeriser, and the almost hideously painful representation of death at the end of the play. The gradual stupefaction, the fixed eye, the head bent down on the chest, and the crouching humility before a stronger will in the one scene; and the very ugly picture of a dead man's face, convulsed after a dream, in which he thought he was hanged, are touches of genuine art, which, while they terrify, cannot fail to be admired. Almost as telling was the low, terrified wail as the awful sentence is being pronounced, and Mathias sinks kneeling to the floor of the court. Vivid and picturesque as is Mr. Irving's art, he somehow failed to convey the genial side of the character of the man. The colouring in the first two acts was of too sombre a tone, and the requisite contrast was, therefore, not given. We believe that M. Talien made his best point by deceiving the audience, and taking it off its guard, by his extreme geniality. Mr. Irving's strength also failed him more than once. The monologue in the dream act is far too long, and Mr. Irving has not the power to carry it through to the entire satisfaction of those in front. The light and shade disappear when the actor has overtaxed his strength. But, taking the bad with the good, the performance is highly satisfactory, and by it, Mr. Irving has unquestionably increased his reputation. In such a character as this, trick and artifice are of no avail. It requires acting out, and cannot be played with. We have no desire to recall our opinion that such a part demands the genius of a Garrick or a Robson; but it is a subject for congratulation that Mr. Irving is able by it to do himself and the Stage such infinite credit. The other characters are comparatively subordinate; but cheerful assistance was given by Miss Pauncefort as the wife; by Mr. Herbert Crellin as the lover, who both looked and acted well; and by Miss Fanny Heywood, who, at the end of the second act, sang the touching 'Air de Rauterbach' [sic] with delightful expression.

Even in these days of scenic splendour and taste in decoration, we seldom see a play so unexceptionally mounted. The interior of the inn in the first act, with its quaint furniture, its shelves of queer crockery, and its thoroughness from end to end, is a picture well worth study; and most striking are the frescoes on the walls of the court of justice, and the general arrangement of this scene. The management has evidently spared no trouble, and grudged no expense, to aid the tragedy and preserve the idyllic character of the story. Messrs. Hawes Craven and Cuthbert are the scenic artistes. The chef d'orchestre of the Théâtre Cluny, M. Singla, has been borrowed from Paris on purpose to conduct and give his assistance in the rehearsals; and with regard to this last subject, we may remark, and it is a point worth noting, that the play was rehearsed to perfection. There was not a hitch or a contretemps of any kind, and it went as well on the first night as it doubtless will when the representations are reckoned by hundreds. Weird enough is the story to be sure, but there is a strange fascination about horrible things, and for many reasons, 'The Bells' is a play, which those interested in the drama as an art should not fail to see. After every act, Mr. Henry Irving was called, and when the usual compliment had been paid to all at the end of the performance, another shout was raised, and Mr. Bateman led on Mr. Irving, shaking him by the hand and patting him on the back. Without a doubt, the audience was much impressed by the new drama.

JOHN OXENFORD IN *THE TIMES*, 28 NOVEMBER 1871

We find a very difficult task very creditably executed in the performance of Mr. H. Irving as the chief personage in an English version of *Le Juif Polonais*, produced on Saturday at the Lyceum, with an extraordinary success to which he, in great measure, contributed. As a valuable actor, especially of bad men in good society, Mr. Irving has for some years been recognized by the London public, and his Digby Grant is perhaps one of the best remembered parts in Mr. Albery's *Two Roses*. But when he appears as a tragic artist, with the duty of sustaining a serious drama single-handed, he may almost be said to make a debut. Decidedly the full measure of his deserts was never known till Saturday last.

Le Juif Polonais, originally written by M.M. Erckmann-Chatrian, more as a dramatic romance than as a drama, was brought out about three years ago at the Théâtre de Cluny, a new house, which, notwithstanding its position on the left bank of the Seine, has acquired a high degree of celebrity. Its success was great, and the clear simplicity of its plot, its appeal to an universal interest, and the great opportunities it afforded to a leading actor at once attracted the attention of English dramatists. There was nothing in the moral distinctively French, no apparent reason why it should not succeed in London as well as in Paris, and had it been brought out ten years ago its transfer to our capital would, doubtless, have been effected with all possible speed. But even before the late war and its consequences had brought Parisian theatricals to a temporary standstill, our authors had begun to draw less liberally than of old upon French resources. Consequently, though *Le Juif Polonais* was much talked about in dramatic circles, and this or that actor was named as likely to give effect to the principal part, it is not till the present winter that any sign of it was manifest on the London boards. Mr. Burnand has founded a piece upon it which, under the name of Paul Zegers, is played at the Alfred Theatre, but his treatment of the subject has been so free that the original idea is therein dimly reflected. The Lyceum version, written by Mr. Leopold Lewis, and entitled *The Bells*, is, if we except one alteration, to all intents and purposes the work of M.M. Erckmann-Chatrian.

The plot, as we have said, is extremely simple, and the interest is purely of a psychological kind, the action of the story in the strict sense of the word having taken place before the rise of the curtain. A man, not of a naturally malignant disposition, but impelled by poverty, has many years ago committed a murder. His character is above suspicion, and the chances that the crime will ever be brought home to him are reduced to a nullity. Nevertheless, his own conscience torments him in form so palpable that it almost becomes a bodily persecution, and he finally dies under its pressure. Such, and no more, is the subject of *Le Juif Polonais*.

Notwithstanding the extreme simplicity the leading idea is so skilfully and carefully developed that three acts are satisfactorily filled. Mathias, burgomaster of an Alsatian town, and likewise an innkeeper, is absent from home when the play begins, and his friends and customers are amusing themselves on Christmas-eve with jests about the approaching marriage of his daughter Annette to Christian, a young gendarme. The coldness of the weather provokes the remark that such severity has been unknown since the 'Polish Jew's winter'. By this Christian's curiosity is aroused. He asks the meaning of the expression, and learns that 15 years ago a Polish Jew who called at the inn mysteriously disappeared shortly after his departure, the horse of his sledge having been found dead and no trace remaining of its owner. At this point of the conversation Mathias comes home, flings off a coat encumbered with snow, presents his daughter with a new hat, after the most approved fashion of Alsace, and seems determined to enjoy the festivities of the season, in which a certain strong white wine is an important ingredient. In the French piece his spirits are dashed by the accidental entrance of a Polish Jew, closely resembling the man murdered years ago. In the English version this incident is omitted, its place being supplied by a sort of vision. Reference to the old Polish Jew has obviously annoyed Mathias, and when he is left alone a jangling of bells is heard, and the scene opening discovers the Jew in a sledge, and the counterpart of Mathias preparing to assail him with a hatchet. This scene, is, of course, supposed to be a creation of conscience, and so is the jangling of the bells which occurs at intervals throughout the piece, and which, though heard by the audience, is understood to be perceptible to Mathias only.

In the second act, which begins on the morning following the vision, Mathias seems to be a good deal shaken, but his infirmity is attributed by the medical man to the effects of the white wine. In truth, he has been distressed not only by the mention of the murder, but by certain mesmeric operations, which, during his absence from home, he has seen performed in a neighbouring town. There a clairvoyant sent a man to sleep, and forced him to reveal his most hidden thoughts. Suppose that he—Mathias—were likewise reduced to a state of coma, what revelations might not ensue! He must be guarded at every point; Christian, the gendarme, will be a good ally in case of danger; so the marriage of Annette shall at once be solemnized, the notary is sent for in a hurry, and the hastily assembled guests admire the magnificence of the Burgomaster, who, on the execution of the contract, lays down 30,000f. in hard cash, as his daughter's portion. Unluckily, while counting over the money alone, his eye has lit upon an old coin, which manifestly belonged to the murdered Jew. Conscience has awakened anew; and while the bridal pair and guests are singing and dancing, the bells once more jangle in his ears, and in his desperate effort to escape the agony they cause, he flings himself into the dance, and disports himself like a maniac till the drop scene falls.

The third act begins on the night of the same day. Mathias is conducted to his chamber by his family and guests, and retiring to his couch has a dream which, visible to the audience, is the principal scene in the play. The stage represents a law court, with three judges seated on the bench, and Mathias arraigned before them on the charge of murder. Frantic with rage and terror he defies all present, declaring that there is no evidence to convict him, till the judges deem it expedient to send for a clairvoyant. He is sent to sleep under the mesmeric influence, a confession of his crime is extorted from him, and when the coma has passed he is horrified to discover that the truth is revealed. He is condemned to death, and at that moment awakes from his dream, to die in the belief that the rope is about his neck. His family and guests gather round him; but, though they are shocked at his untimely end, they have no reason to suspect its terrible cause.

It will be obvious to every reader that the efficiency of this singular play depends almost wholly upon the actor who represents Mathias. To this one part all the others are subordinate, and while it is most grateful to an artist who can appreciate and grapple with its difficulties, it would altogether crush an aspirant whose ambition was disproportionate to his talent; but, remarkable for the strength of his physique, Mr. H. Irving has thrown the whole force of his mind into the character, and works out bit by bit the concluding hours of a life passed in a constant effort to preserve a cheerful exterior with a conscience tortured till it has become a monomania. It is a marked peculiarity of the moral position of Mathias that he has no confidant, that he is not subjected to the extortions of some mercenary wretch who would profit by his knowledge. He is at once in two worlds, between which there is no link—an outer world that is ever smiling, an inner world which is a purgatory. Hence a dreaminess in his manner, which Mr. Irving accurately represents in his frequent transitions from a display of the domestic affections to the fearful work of self-communion. In the dream his position is changed. The outer world is gone, and conscience is all triumphant, assisted by an imagination which violently brings together the anticipated terrors of a criminal court and the mesmeric feats he has recently witnessed. The struggles of the miserable culprit, convinced that all is lost, but desperately fighting against hope, rebelling against the judges, protesting against the clairvoyant, who wrings his secret from him, are depicted by Mr. Irving with a degree of energy that, fully realizing the horror of the situation, seems to hold the audience in suspense. On Saturday it was not till the curtain fell, and they summoned the actor before it with a storm of acclamation, that they seemed to recover their self-possession. Nevertheless, so painful is the interest of the scene that, notwithstanding the excellent manner in which it is played, we would suggest its reduction to a smaller compass.

The piece is put upon the stage with admirable completeness, the smaller parts being adequately sustained, Messrs. H. Craven and Cuthbert having painted most appropriate scenery, and the original melo-dramatic music being brought from Paris by its composer, M. E. Singlar [sic], who conducts the orchestra with the permission of M. Larochelle, the manager of the Théâtre de Cluny.

AN UNSIGNED REVIEW IN *THE DAILY TELEGRAPH*, 8 NOVEMBER 1887

In considering the performance by M. Coquelin of Mathis in *Le Juif Polonais*
we must never forget that he is not playing the weird and romantic drama
The Bells, as Mr. Irving has made us understand it, but is following in the
footsteps of M. Talien, who, so far back as June, 1869, drew public attention
at the little Cluny Theatre to the dramatic version of the story by M.M.
Erckmann-Chatrian. The Mathis of this simple Alsatian story, as M. Coquelin
understands him, is anything but a picturesque personage. He is a rotund,
bright-eyed, commonplace little fellow; a miniature L'Ami Fritz without his
polish and deep-seated imagination. It is part of the authors' scheme to present
to us a man with two lives; to show us how an ordinary Alsatian innkeeper,
affectionate to his family, beloved by his friends, the most respected man in
the neighbourhood, can, when alone, be troubled with a disagreeable thing
called conscience, and he harassed with the thought of a murder committed
by him years before, which very crime, by the acquisition of stolen property,
was the foundation-stone of his prosperity. But Erckmann-Chatrian are very
particular to insist that from the beginning of the play to the end no one except
the audience is to know a word about the guilt of Mathis. We who look on
read his mind, watch his apprehension, are witnesses of his dreams and night-
mares; but the family of the murderer think to the end that his death has been
caused by persisting in drinking too much white wine, and that his last moments
have been painless and peaceable. Says the Doctor, when the collapse has come,
'C'est fini! M. le Bourgmestre est mort. Le vin blanc l'a tué.' Says the faithful
son-in-law, 'Quel malheur! un si brave homme!' Says his oldest friend, with
a sign of relief, 'C'est la plus belle mort. On ne souffre pas.' Anxious to impress
these simple truths upon his audience, M. Coquelin seems to us to go out of
his way to realise the prosaic old innkeeper at the expense of the picturesque-
ness of the play. Mr. Irving conceived a man whose nerves were unhinged by
the action of awakened conscience; M. Coquelin sketches a cheery little old
gentleman, who chuckles to himself that he has hoodwinked his neighbours
and cheated the law. All the detail of the home-life of the Alsatian innkeeper
is admirably sketched by the French actor; to all outward appearance he is
the man he personates; but surely it would have considerably enhanced the
interest of the play if, without over-accentuating the well-known dramatic
points, he had given colour and added force to his soliloquies and to the cele-
brated dream scene. The English actor used the story to show us how an evil
conscience can unnerve and fret a man; the French actor insists that by an
unimaginative mind and unsensitive nature the twinges of uncomfortable recollection can be comparatively ignored. According to M. Coquelin's idea the entrance of Mathis should be undemonstrative and ineffective. It is only a simple
old fellow coming home from a fair in Alsatia, so why make a fuss about it?
When he tells his family that he has seen a mountebank who sends men to
sleep and reads their minds, this uncomfortable fact does not seem to awake
the slightest suspicion, or in any way trouble the merry little fellow. His face

betrays no sudden flash of recollection. Even when the name of the Polish Jew is mentioned there is only one quick change of expression which is instantaneously followed by a chuckle. The dream bells jingle, but the stolid countenance remains immovable. It is only when the duplicated Polish Jew comes into the inn that Mathis utters one sharp and sudden cry, not of terror but of pain. His friends and the good doctor think it is only an indigestion pang—that he has taken too much white wine. But if the first act, that elsewhere we have found to be so varied, so absorbing, and so full of interest, be comparatively tame and uneventful, what shall be said of the colourlessness of the second?

We say to ourselves, let M. Coquelin only be left alone on the stage, and he will become a totally different man. Not a bit of it. He goes on chuckling with his conscience, not wrestling with it. He hugs himself with delight that there are such fools in the world, but apparently he has no apprehension. The scene with the money-bags, how tame—the discovery of the bit of gold left from the robbery, how it is slurred over! Mathis puts the blood-money into his pocket without so much as a shudder. Who can forget the agonised look of Mr. Irving when he separated the bloodstained coin from the marriage portion? Again, in the scene with Christian, who is getting gradually near the truth, there is no change of expression, nothing to indicate what the old man is thinking of, except that he is a remarkably clever fellow who will hoodwink even the conscientious young officer. In the gay scene of the marriage contract, with its old song and dance, there is no attempt to bring Mathis into the front group of the picture. The bells—and dreadfully bad bells they are, by the way—ring in the ears of the burgomaster; but he apparently heeds them not, as he dances behind the stove when the curtain falls upon a succession of scenes pretty enough in their way, but destitute of significance. Necessarily there must be a change in the last act. It is impossible to play the dream scene in the same unimaginative, uneventful fashion. Here M. Coquelin showed some power, but little variety; he was alternately angry and lachrymose; he was savage and weak. He enacted the murder with some attempt at vigorous treatment, but when the curtain fell finally it was felt that, purposely or not, the actor had neglected to observe the psychology of the play, had cast from his consideration all notion of a conscience-haunted man, had refused to unbare his mind even to his audience, but preferred to show us what a somewhat commonplace little Alsatian burgomaster would do if he were suddenly confronted with the recollection of a crime that does not apparently weigh very heavily on such mind as he possesses.

INTRODUCTION TO THE MUSIC

MUSIC TO MELODRAMA

There are many definitions of the theatrical genre melodrama. Some of these definitions proceed from melodrama's recurring structural characteristics. Other definitions, disagreeing, follow from the alleged psychological or social or emotional character or effects of these plays. All definitions are in accord on one point, that melodrama involves the use of emotive music accompanying dialogue that is not sung but spoken, and that music also accompanies physical action to heighten the emotional colour of the drama. In respect that it employs music to draw audience attention to emotional qualities which the producers of these dramas hope to stress, melodrama bears a notional resemblance to opera. Such a superficial similarity is not surprising, for indeed a species of popular opera, the so-called 'rescue' or 'escape' opera which emerged in the Parisian theatres in the last decades of the eighteenth century, may have inspired or at the very least coincided with the early melodrama which developed in the Paris environment. After the French Revolution the number of theatres in France increased rapidly, producing a new type of drama about class struggle, employing sensations, spectacles, violence and an underlying current of pathos. Some of these pieces, the work of such innovators as René Charles Guilbert de Pixérecourt, were entitled *melo-drames*, whilst other works produced by the composers Cherubini and Lesurieur were offered as opera. Yet the structural, dramatic and musical distinctions between early *melodrame* and such opera are slight.

Cherubini's operas include *Lodoiska* (1791), *Les Deux Journees* (1800), and *Faniska* (1806). These operas have spoken dialogue linking the musical numbers. The plots are full of violent events, suspense, danger, emotion and a last-minute rescue. Class division is an ingredient in the dramatic conflict, and the rights of oppressed people over the tyranny of their superiors is expressed with great emotion. The libretti, therefore, had a new direct appeal to the audience in that they were not about remote or allegoric characters but about 'real' people identifiable with themselves. English adaptations of French melodrama and rescue drama obliterated fine distinctions in nomenclature. Henceforeward, all serious drama thus accompanied by music was melodrama, and, soon, musical hacks and such rising composers as Henry Bishop alike supplied theatres with melodramatic music ranging from full scores to segments of music designated 'hurries', 'agits' (agitatos) and 'mists' (mysteriosos).

A fresh inspiration to the music of melodrama came from the composer Carl Maria von Weber. In 1824 Weber's *Der Freischütz* was produced at Covent Garden and offered audiences, albeit in somewhat elevated terms, elements by that date associated with melodrama: scenes of humble but happy village life, a pure maid and heroine, a well-intentioned but gullible hero, a villain who gets caught in his own trap, and a range of supernatural occurrences. Moreover, the music also has elements which thereafter make up the many clichés of melo- dramatic music: diminished seventh chords, tremolo strings, pizzicato basses and rumbling kettledrums. In the 'Wolf's Glen' scene which ends Act II, Weber used many devices that are found in subsequent melodramas including mysteri- ous harmonies on tremolo strings, unison playing, the spoken voice over music, and folk-song-like melodies side by side with more conventional operatic arias. One of the outstanding features of the opera is the unity given by the repetition of themes throughout.

Even before the 1870s and the beginnings of Irving's tenure at the Lyceum, the practice of musical support for serious drama had encountered adverse criti- cism. Opponents of music objected to the triteness of the music or to the ease with which audiences' emotional responses could be so easily anticipated and manipulated with a few bars of melody. Some of the critics of such music were its composers, and one composer of theatre music, Norman O'Neill, has left his views on record. In a paper presented in 1911 to the Musical Association (later to become The Royal Musical Association), O'Neill states,

> I should like to mention Hatton's music written for Charles Kean's Shakespearean and other productions in the 'fifties'. These were, as far as I know, the first produc- tions of modern times in England in which a well-known musician of the day was specially engaged to write special music for a play. This has in our own day become a regular practice. Most of our composers have written music for plays at some time or other. It is to Sir Henry Irving, who did so much to improve the artistic conditions of the theatre, we are indebted for this. He saw the need of something better than the so-called 'hurries', 'tremolos', and sentimental hymn-like tunes which were being served up again and again in our theatres to an easily imposed- upon public.[1]

O'Neill goes on to classify the music used in the theatre under three headings:

> The first:—Incidental music—which may or may not be specially composed for the play. The second:—Entr'actes and interlude music. The third:—Music which is specially written for a play, and which is an essential part of the production.

In the first category O'Neill has placed the music to melodrama, and states:

> Here the music plays a subsidiary part. It usually accompanies the most sentimental passages in the play, and plays a part similar to that of the limelight man, following the hero and heroine most obstinately. But the villain too will also have his little bit of *tremolo* to help him along on his evil path. This type is usually most primitive in construction. It consists of an eight-bar phrase repeated *ad libitum* during a

speech. And this proceeding will take place many times during an evening, so that it is very often heard forty or fifty times in the course of a play. Its use, if it can be so-called, is usually to remind the audience of a previous situation. When the hero lies in prison, for instance, memories of the 'old home' and his first meeting with the heroine are called up, and of course the old tune turns up too.

O'Neill is scathing about the effectiveness of this type of recall through music and its use to 'bolster up the weakness of the drama'. With constant repetition of trite themes this complaint is wholly justified. However, O'Neill exempts Irving's Lyceum dramas on the ground that Irving cut so much superfluous music in his productions that music became an essential part of the whole, and not merely incidental. O'Neill does, however, conclude the section on incidental music with this statement: 'It is not always so much the intrinsic value of the music so much as its appropriateness and aptness which make it successful from the theatrical point of view.' When music is to accompany speech, O'Neill writes:

> To my mind music which accompanies the spoken words should be as unobtrusive as possible and not, strictly speaking, melodic. The feeling of the words should be followed more in the general harmonic scheme than by any clear-cut melody. An apt chord or turn of phrase is often more suggestive than a defined melody, which is often distracting when accompanying the spoken lines. The musical accompaniment to a speech should steal in and steal out so quietly, that the audience are no more aware of it than they are of some subtle change in the stage lighting. Bizet is most successful in his treatment of the melodrama in 'L'Arlesienne', the music often beginning with one or two pianissimo violin notes *con sordini* and fading away again in the same way. I do not wish to give you the impression that in music for the stage melody has no place. On the contrary, no successful incidental music (or any other for that matter) can be devoid of melody and thematic material. I only feel that clearly defined tunes in conjunction with the dialogue are out of place.

Finally, O'Neill discusses the kind of orchestra found in the Victorian and Edwardian theatres.

> This brings me to the vexed question of what is the best orchestral combination to use in the theatre. There are two difficulties, one of which it is practically impossible to overcome viz., the long narrow shape of the theatre orchestra pit; the other being the limited space at one's disposal. There are few theatres where it is possible to seat more than thirty players comfortably. And it must be borne in mind that twenty-six players with elbow-room will probably give you a better effect than thirty players cramped and packed close together. Personally, I very much object to an orchestra in which there are as many wind players as strings. So often in the theatre, music is played which has been scored for an orchestra of at least fifty with three trombones, trumpets, horns and full wood-wind, against which struggle seven or eight violins, two violas, and two violoncellos. To my mind, it is far better to do with less wind and brass, and to get something like a proper balance between wind and strings. I will not lay down any hard and fast rule, but for ordinary purposes an orchestra of, say, twenty-six performers should, I think, be constituted in this way:

4 first violins	2 flutes
3 second violins	1 oboe
2 violas	2 clarinets
2 violoncellos	1 bassoon
2 double-basses	2 horns, 2 trumpets,

and one trombone or harp and celesta (one player), one percussion.

This at any rate, to my mind is the minimum of string players possible with this amount of wind, and even then they must be first-rate performers, and must have no dummies amongst them. The harp is more essential in a small orchestra than in a large one. It makes just this difference, I think, it turns what we call a 'theatre band' into a little orchestra.

But twenty-six performers are a comparative luxury. For a run of a play in which there is no music, and during which the orchestra is only required in the entr' actes, a conductor may consider himself lucky if his management allows him eighteen or even sixteen players. For ordinary purposes an orchestra of eighteen performers should be constituted thus:

4 first violins	1 oboe
2 second violins	1 clarinet
1 viola	1 bassoon
2 violoncellos	2 horns
1 bass	1 trumpet
1 flute	

and percussion. Of course with only a small orchestra the conductor will find it necessary to arrange nearly all the standard works, and in many cases practically re-score them for his combination of instruments. Many good arrangements of works by the great masters are published, but in numerous cases they fall short of the ideal, as the publishers insist that they be arranged in such a way that they can be played with some degree of effect by six or eighty performers.

THE SCORE FOR *THE BELLS*

The music of *The Bells* was written by Etienne Singla. Little is known of Singla's life or other works apart from the music used for *Le Juif Polonais* which was produced in 1869 at the Théâtre Cluny, where Singla was musical director. The only other works he is known to have composed are a 'Tarentelle' for piano and incidental music for George Sand's drama *Claudie* which was produced about 1870 at the Théâtre de l'Odeon, Paris. Singla was invited to England by Colonel Bateman to conduct the first performance of *The Bells* at the Lyceum Theatre, London, on 25 November 1871.

During the years that *The Bells* was performed by Irving, he made, as we have seen, constant revisions to the text of the play, changing words and phrases and deleting parts of the script as necessary. He altered the music in a similar manner. Many pieces of incidental music were cut by Irving, as in his view they contributed little to the continuity and unity of the drama.

In most melodramas of the time, the entrance of each character was introduced by a piece of incidental music. However in *The Bells*, Irving has cut out the entrance music of all but the most significant characters in the plot—namely Mathias and the Mesmerist. Thus, by deletions, has Irving emphasised the role of Mathias, and all the music that is left—with the exception of the overture, certain dance music and the drinking song—has a direct relationship and significance to Mathias. In Act I music is cued for the entrance of both Annette and Christian (Ex. 1), but both pieces were cut by Irving presumably as they bear no great significance to the characterisation of Mathias.

Example 1   *Christian's Entrance Music*   Cue: 'No! No! It is Christian.'

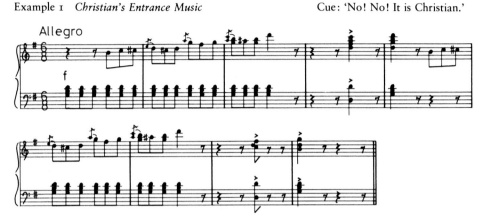

The score printed here was passed from Henry Irving to his son, H. B. Irving, from H. B. Irving to Henry Baynton, from Henry Baynton to Martin-Harvey, and from Martin-Harvey to Eric Jones-Evans. Several copies have been made over the years. The piano reduction printed here does not include all the music that was used in the first production of *The Bells* but is, nevertheless, the music that Irving used in his later productions.

Orchestral parts which survive are the piano/conductor score and one each of the other parts: violin I, violin II, viola, 'cello, double bass, flute, clarinet, cornets, trombone and percussion (kettledrums, side drums, bass drum and bells). The piano/conductor part is a reduction of the full score for keyboard. Irving is known to have had a piano reduction of the music in his orchestral parts. The surviving piano reduction is probably a copy of Irving's. His various conductors either used a piano/conductor score or read from a copy of the violin I part. The combination of instruments used in the score to *The Bells* is typical of the theatre orchestras of the day.

In practice, the number of players used in the orchestra varied from theatre to theatre. The orchestra at the Lyceum Theatre numbered about twenty-six players divided thus: six first violins, six second violins, three violas, three 'cellos, one double bass, one flute, one clarinet, two cornets, one trombone and two percussionists. This orchestra would provide a well-balanced and adequate sound. On tour and in smaller theatres, however, neither the size of the pit nor that of the resident orchestra was up to the standard of the Lyceum. In touring, therefore, Irving had to accept whatever he found. Only in the case of a very small or inadequate orchestra would the piano part be played.

In the score, the strings form the main body of the orchestra. The orchestration is simple, straightforward and uncomplicated and special colours are seldom used.

OVERTURE

The overture, like most nineteenth-century operatic overtures, incorporates many of the themes which recur throughout the play, thereby establishing motifs for the action which is to follow. Some of the seven sections are very short, and the whole overture lasts only about five minutes. The second section introduces the sound of the sleigh bells which torment Mathias throughout the play. Another section is used as the curtain music for Act I, and the theme of the Drinking Song of Act II makes up the penultimate section.

The overture itself is not a unified piece of music such as would be expected in the operatic overture of the time, but it does help to create the mood of the drama. Forceful sections with great rhythmic drive create feelings of suspense and tension and are offset by quieter lilting themes, the whole creating an anticipatory mood.

ACT I

When the curtain rises on Act I the scene is of the Burgomaster's Inn and the music enhances the quiet domestic scene. Later, the conversation turns to Mathias's return and the appalling weather. The music that heralds the arrival of Mathias is a short 'hurry' of six bars which increases in speed and volume until Mathias bursts through the door on the final chord with the famous line 'It is I!'

Mathias gives Annette a wedding present of a necklace and during the brief but touching scene in which she unwraps the gift, a soft piece of music played by strings alone. The piece conjures up the feelings of love and tenderness that Mathias has for his daughter. These emotions become heightened during the play with the repetition of this theme especially when the control Mathias has over his mind diminishes and his impatience for his daughter's marriage increases. This is the principal theme used in the music of Act III.

With the striking of the clock the final music of Act I is heard. In this scene good use is made of 'melodramatic' tremolo writings for strings. The use of tremolo strings over a pizzicato bass creates an amazing feeling of tension. Mathias rushes about the stage trying to block out the sound of the sleigh bells. With the sight of the vision, the bells, wind and music increase in volume, until finally Mathias collapses with a shriek and the curtain falls.

ACT II

Act II is concerned with the preparations for the marriage of Annette and Christian. The audience now know of Mathias's dilemma. He is outwardly smiling and jovial whilst inwardly he is in torment lest his secret should be revealed before the wedding. He feels he will be safe after the wedding as Christian would defend him if anything were to be revealed about the murder of the Jew.

When the curtain rises on Act II, two days have elapsed and a doctor is in attendance on Mathias. Mathias assures the doctor that he is now better. The music that takes up the curtain on Act II is more peaceful. It is a lilting, almost pastoral piece, reminiscent of the music associated with Annette in Act I. As this second act is mainly concerned with the preparations for Annette's wedding, the music with similarity to that of Act I provides a unity between the two acts.

After the doctor leaves, Annette enters and the music associated with her is heard again. Here the scoring is slightly thinner in that there is no viola part, but the feeling conveyed of Mathias's deep affection for his daughter is the same. This emotion is evoked once more in this act when Mathias is counting the dowry. Annette's theme is played as Mathias remembers how, without the money, he would have been ruined. Now, however, the music is transformed by a chromatic bass line which mirrors the increasing uneasiness felt by Mathias. Annette's music is truncated and the 'mysterioso' piece from the end of Act I is tacked on to the end. With the mysterioso section the bells are heard again, and once more the feelings of anticipation and suspense about the final fate of Mathias are felt.

With the completion of the final preparations for the signing of the wedding contract, the villagers are invited to witness the event. As they enter, a small band off stage consisting of violin, double bass, cornet, trombone and drums plays the first refrain of the 'Lauterbach'. The music in the score is for full orchestra because the Lauterbach was originally played from the pit, with the small band playing on the stage. On tour, owing to the varying sizes of acting area, it was sometimes necessary to have the musicians off stage. This allowed more room for villagers and so prompted Irving to move the band off stage and even to revert to the pit orchestra.

When the contract is signed, Mathias calls for a waltz before dinner. The pit orchestra strikes up the first chord when Father Walter cries, 'Stop! Stop! Let's first hear the Song of Betrothal!' With cheers of agreement from the others, the Lauterbach is played again to accompany Annette's singing of the song. The melody of the Lauterbach is probably better known in the popular version that appeared soon after the original production with the words, 'Oh vere and oh vere is my leetle dog gone.' Mathias is relieved because the contract has now been signed. After the aside, 'And now if the Jew should return Christian must drive him back again', he feels he is safe and danger has been averted. However when the waltzing is at its height Mathias again hears the bells and terror once more assails him. Rushing wildly among the dancers he cries, 'The Bells! The Bells', and he seizes his wife by the waist, waltzes round madly and defiantly shouts, 'Ring on. Ring on to hell'. As he does so, the music and bells increase in volume to stop abruptly as the curtain falls for the end of the act.

ACT III

With the rise of the curtain on Act III, the music is an arrangement for full orchestra of the drinking song heard later in the act as the revellers leave the Inn. The scene is Mathias's bedroom on the same night. There is much gaiety and laughter off stage. After Mathias has been wished goodnight by all the guests, he says goodnight to Catherine and Annette. This parting is accompanied very faintly by Annette's theme. Left alone, Mathias prepares for bed as the revellers depart singing the Drinking Song in a very spasmodic, drunken fashion (Ex. 2).

Example 2 *Drinking Song*

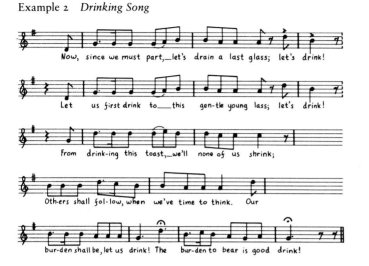

Now, since we must part,—let's drain a last glass; let's drink!

Let us first drink to—this gen-tle young lass; let's drink!

From drink-ing this toast,—we'll none of us shrink;

Oth-ers shall fol-low, when we've time to think. Our

bur-den shall be, let us drink! The bur-den to bear is good drink!

Mathias now retires to bed and snuffs out the candle to the accompaniment of a gentle lullaby. His slumbers are not to be peaceful as he is disturbed by vivid dreams of a court in which he is on trial for the murder of the Polish Jew. Nothing in the court is seen clearly except for Mathias. Everything is of a blue, misty, dream-like character, and against the grey walls of the court, voices fade in and out as the direction of questioning alters.

The mesmerist who is summoned to the court to send Mathias to sleep is the only character in the play besides Mathias to have entrance music. His music is for unison strings and clarinet and has a theme typical of sinister, melodramatic happenings. The mesmerist is asked to put Mathias into a trance, which he does to music (Ex. 3). This music slows and fades as Mathias tries to resist the mesmerist but finally succumbs.

Example 3 *Mathias is made to sleep*

Andante

No No I will not sleep I ... will ... not ... sleep

rall.

I will not sl . . . . (breathes deeply)

Mathias re-enacts the murder of the Jew in his state of trance and is sentenced to death by the court. With the sentence, a death bell tolls and the music is played slowly and smoothly. This music does not evoke a feeling of just reward for the terrible crime committed, but of sympathy for Mathias because he acted as he did to save his wife and himself from ruin and to secure a good future for his daughter.

With repeated knocks at the bedroom door, the lights go up to reveal the bedroom on the next morning. It is Annette's wedding day and a peal of church bells can be heard in the middle distance. Annette's theme is heard at the mention of her wedding day. The door is broken down and Mathias staggers on to the stage gasping for breath, tugging at an imaginary rope around his neck. The sleigh bells jingle until he dies, and at this point the last four bars of music are played *fortissimo* as the curtain descends.

MUSIC CUES

Irving cut much music from the original score of *The Bells*, just as he altered or cut many words and paragraphs from the original script by Leopold Lewis. To clarify the points at which Irving left the music intact, the following list of cues and directions may be of assistance:

Overture   *Allegro vivo*

Act I

No. 1   *Andante*
    To take up the curtain
    Fade out at the curtain

No. 2   *Moderato*
    Cue: Walter: 'Well he deserves all the success he has achieved.'
    Play once. Crescendo to entrance of Mathias.

No. 3   *Andante*
    Cue: Annette: 'Thank you, dear father. How good you are.'
    Play softly. Fade out at
    Cue: Mathias: 'My only hope is to see you happy with Christian.'

No. 4   *Andante mysterioso*
    Cue: Mathias: 'Ten o'clock. The very hour.'
    Repeat *pianissimo* until Mathias shrieks and falls, then straight on to coda *fortissimo* to the curtain.

Act II

No. 5   *Andante dolce*
    To take up the curtain.
    Fade out at the curtain.

No. 6   *Andante*
    Cue: Annette: 'Yes, I've finished at last. I'm sorry to have kept you waiting, mother.'
    Play once, *pianissimo*, muted.

No. 7   *Andante Mysterioso*
    Cue: Mathias: 'Without it we should've been ruined.'
    Play Andante section dolce and coincide
    Mysterioso on cue: 'The Bells—the bells again!"
    Repeat mysterioso section to stop on
    Cue: Sozel: 'No, Burgomaster, I heard nothing.'

No. 8   *Allegro (Lauterbach)*
Small band off stage.
Cue: Mathias: 'It is an old but honest custom of Alsace.'
Repeat and stop when Notary speaks.

No. 9   *Song of Betrothal (Lauterbach)*
Chord after cue:
Mathias: '... one waltz, and then to supper.'
Song after cue: Walter: 'Stop! Stop! Let's first have the Song of Betrothal!'
Repeat the last twelve bars *piano* until
Cue: Mathias: 'Ring on! Ring on!'
then accelerando and crescendo to curtain. No chord.

Act III

No. 10   *Allegro vivo*
To take up the curtain.

No. 11   *Andante*
Cue: At exit of guests.
Repeat last eight bars if necessary.
Fade out at Catherine's exit.

No. 12   *Andante maestoso*
Cue: At snuffing out of candle.
Repeat last four bars as necessary.
Fade out at scene.

No. 13   *Marked and emphatic*
Cue: Mathias: 'Come and defend me!'
Play twice; first time loud, second time fading away.

No. 14   *Andante mysterioso*
Cue: Mathias: 'If you sleep you are lost!'
Play once.

No. 15   *Largo—vivo*
Cue: President: '... hanged by the neck until he is dead.'
Play first four bars pianissimo until
Lights up.
Play last two bars vivo until knocking at door.

No. 16   *Andante*
Cue: Catherine: 'It's Annette's wedding day.'
Repeat last four bars as necessary, slowing and fading as Mathias dies.
At death, repeat last four bars *fortissimo* to end the play.

NOTE

1. This statement and subsequent quotations from Norman O'Neill, *Proceedings of the Royal Musical Association*, 1910–11, pp. 85–102.

OVERTURE *THE BELLS*

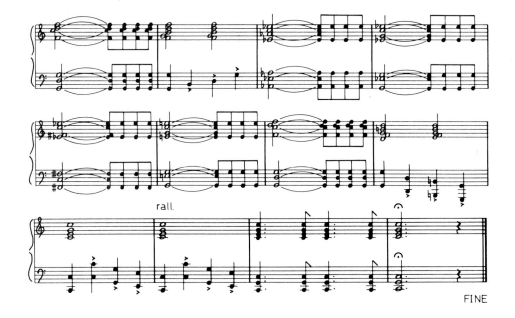

FINE

ACT 1, NO. 1

To take up the curtain.
Fade out at the curtain.

ACT 1, NO. 2

Cue: WALTER   Well he deserves all the success he has achieved.
Play once. Crescendo to entrance of MATHIAS.

ACT 1, NO. 3

Cue: ANNETTE   Thank you, dear father. How good you are.
Play softly. Fade out at ...
Cue: MATHIAS   My only hope is to see you happy with Christian.

ACT II, NO. 4

Cue: MATHIAS   Ten o'clock. The very hour.

Repeat pianissimo until Mathias shrieks and falls, then straight on to coda fortissimo to the curtain.

ACT II, NO. 5

To take up the curtain.
Fade out at the curtain.

ACT II, NO. 6

Cue: ANNETTE   Yes, I've finished at last. I'm sorry to have kept you
waiting, Mother.

Play once, pianissimo, muted.

ACT II, NO. 7

Cue: MATHIAS   Without it we should've been ruined.

Play Andante section dolce and coincide

Mysterioso on cue: 'The Bells—the bells again!'

Repeat· mysterioso section to stop on cue

    SOZEL   No, Burgomaster, I heard nothing.

ACT II, NO. 8 *Allegro (Lauterbach)*

Small band off stage.
Cue: MATHIAS   It is an old but honest custom of Alsace.
Repeat and stop when Notary speaks.

ACT II, NO. 9 *Song of Betrothal (Lauterbach)*

CHORD after cue:
MATHIAS   … one waltz, and then to supper.
Song after cue: WALTER   Stop! Stop! Let's first have the Song of Betrothal!

Repeat the last 12 bars piano until cue: MATHIAS   Ring on! Ring on!
then accelerando and crescendo to curtain. No chord. Stop dead.

ACT III, NO. 10

To take up the curtain.

ACT III, NO. 11

Cue: At exit of guests.
Repeat last 8 bars if necessary.
Fade out at Catherine's exit.

ACT III, NO. 12

Cue: At snuffing out of candle.
Repeat last 4 bars as necessary.
Fade out at scene.

ACT III, NO. 13

Cue: MATHIAS   Come and defend me!
Play twice; first time loud, second time fading away.

ACT III, NO. 14

Cue: MATHIAS   If you sleep you are lost!
Play once.

ACT III, NO. 15

Cue: PRESIDENT ... hanged by the neck until he is dead.
Play first 4 bars pianissimo until lights up.
Play last 2 bars vivo until knocking at door.

ACT III, NO. 16

Cue: CATHERINE It's Annette's wedding day.
Repeat last 4 bars as necessary, slowing and fading as MATHIAS dies.
At death, repeat last 4 bars fortissimo to end the play.

SELECTED BIBLIOGRAPHY

HENRY IRVING AND HENRY BRODRIBB (H. B.) IRVING

ARTHUR WILLIAM A'BECKETT, *Green-Room Recollections*, Bristol and London, 1896.

J. H. BARNES, *Forty Years on the Stage: Others (Principally) and Myself*, London, 1914.

AUSTIN BRERETON, *Henry Irving, A Biographical Sketch*, London, 1883.

—— *The Lyceum and Henry Irving*, London, 1903.

—— *Henry Irving*, London, 1905.

—— *'H.B.' and Lawrence Irving*, London, 1922.

EDWARD GORDON CRAIG, *Henry Irving*, London, 1930.

WALTER CALVERT, *Souvenir of Henry Irving*, London, 1896.

PERCY FITZGERALD, *Henry Irving, A Record of Twenty Years at the Lyceum*, London, 1893.

JOSEPH HATTON, *Henry Irving's Impressions of America: Narrated in a Series of Sketches, Chronicles, and Conversations*, 2 vols., London, 1884.

CHARLES HIATT, *Henry Irving, A Record and Review*, London, 1899.

LAURENCE IRVING, *Henry Irving, The Actor and His World*, London, 1951.

—— *The Successors*, London, 1967.

—— *The Precarious Crust*, 1971.

WALTER HERRIES POLLOCK, *Impressions of Henry Irving*, London, 1908.

H. A. SAINTSBURY AND CECIL PALMER (eds.), *We Saw Him Act, A Symposium on the Art of Sir Henry Irving*, London, 1939.

CLEMENT SCOTT, *From 'The Bells' to 'King Arthur'*, London, 1896.

—— *The Drama of Yesterday and Today*, 2 vols. London, 1899.

—— *Thirty Years at the Play: Dramatic Table Talk*, London, 1890.

GEORGE R. SIMS, *My Life: Sixty Years' Recollections of Bohemian London*, London, 1917.

—— *Glances Back*, London, 1917.

BRAM STOKER, *Personal Reminiscences of Henry Irving*, 2 vols., London, 1906.

ELLEN TERRY, with EDITH CRAIG and CHRISTOPHER ST JOHN, *Ellen Terry's Memoirs*, London, 1933.

H. M. WALBROOK, *A Playgoer's Wanderings*, London, 1926.

FREEMAN WILLS, *W. G. Wills, Dramatist and Painter*, London, 1898.

M. E. WOTTON, *H. B. Irving*, London, 1912.

JOHN MARTIN-HARVEY

GEORGE EDGAR, *Martin Harvey, Some Pages of his Life*, London, 1912.

'R.N.G.-A.' [Richard N. Greene-Armytage], *The Book of Martin Harvey*, London, 1928.

JOHN MARTIN-HARVEY, *The Autobiography of Sir John Martin-Harvey*, London, 1933.

MAURICE WILLSON-DISHER, *The Last Romantic*, London, 1951.

HENRY BAYNTON

H. CHANCE NEWTON, *Cues and Curtain Calls*, London, 1927.
—— *Crime and the Drama*, London, 1927.

BRANSBY WILLIAMS

BRANSBY WILLIAMS, *An Actor's Story*, London, 1909.
—— *Bransby Williams, by Himself*, London, 1954.

MODERN ANTHOLOGIES OF NINETEENTH-CENTURY PLAYS CONTAINING THE SAMUEL FRENCH EDITION OF *THE BELLS*.

LEONARD R. N. ASHLEY (ed.), *Nineteenth Century British Drama*, Glenview, U.S.A.

MICHAEL R. BOOTH (ed.), *English Plays of the Nineteenth Century*, vol. II, *Drama 1850–1900*, Oxford, 1969.
—— *Hiss the Villain*, London, 1964.

GEORGE ROWELL (ed.), *Nineteenth Century Plays*, Oxford, 1963.

MUSIC FOR *THE BELLS*

JAMES LEGGIO, 'Irving and Chaliapin', *Theatre Notebook*, XXXII, 1 (1978) pp. 32—7.

DAVID MAYER, '19th Century Theatre Music', *Theatre Notebook*, XXX, 3 (1976) pp. 115–22.
—— 'The Music of Melodrama', in *Performance and Popular Drama: Aspects of Popular Entertainment in Theatre Film and Television, 1800–1976* (ed. David Bradby, Louis James, and Bernard Sharratt), Cambridge University Press, 1980, pp. 49–63.

NORMAN O'NEILL, 'Music to Stage Plays', *Proceedings for the Royal Musical Association, 1910–1911*, pp. 85–102.

FILMS WITH SEQUENCES FROM *THE BELLS*

The Film and Television Unit of the Department of Drama, University of Bristol, have produced two colour films in which Dr Jones-Evans re-enacts moments from Irving's production of *The Bells*: 'Eric Jones-Evans, Man of the Theatre', 40 minutes, colour, 16 mm, directed by Michael Hall; 'Edwardian Acting: Eric Jones-Evans in conversation with Richard Briers', 20 minutes, colour, 16 mm, directed by Michael Hall. Both films are available on hire, and videotapes of the films may be purchased from the Audio-visual Aid Unit, Department of Drama, University of Bristol, 29 Park Row, Bristol BS1 5LT.

AUDIO CASSETTE OF *THE BELLS*

Michael Hall has also produced an audio cassette of the Samuel French edition of *The Bells* with Eric Jones-Evans as Mathias. This cassette may also be purchased from the address above.